DRIVE

The VIRAT KOHLI Story

CW00435298

DRIVEN
The VIRAT KOHLI Story

VIJAY LOKAPALLY

B L O O M S B U R Y
NEW DELHI • LONDON • OXFORD • NEW YORK • SYDNEY

© *Vijay Lokapally,* 2016

First published, 2016
This export edition published 2017

All rights reserved. No part of this publication may be reproduced or transmitted in any form or by any means, electronic or mechanical, including photocopying, recording, or any information storage or retrieval system, without prior permission in writing from the copyright holder.

No responsibility for loss caused to any individual or organization acting on or refraining from action as a result of the material in this publication can be accepted by Bloomsbury India or the author.

BLOOMSBURY PUBLISHING INDIA PVT. LTD.
New Delhi London Oxford New York Sydney

ISBN: 978-93-86250-63-6

10 9 8 7 6 5

Published by Bloomsbury Publishing India Pvt. Ltd.
DDA Complex LSC, Building No. 4, 2nd Floor
Pocket 6 & 7, Sector C
Vasant Kunj, New Delhi 110070

Cover designed by Graficus

Printed and bound in India

The content of this book is the sole expression and opinion of its authors, and not of the publishers. The publisher in no manner is liable for any opinion or views expressed by the authors. While best efforts have been made in preparing this book, the publishers makes no representations or warranties of any kind and assumes no liabilities of any kind with respect to the accuracy or completeness of the content and specifically disclaims any implied warranties of merchant ability or fitness of use of a particular purpose.

The publisher believes that the contents of this book do not violate any existing copyright/intellectual property of others in any manner whatsoever. However, in case any source has not been duly attributed, the publisher may be notified in writing for necessary action.

For

Aai and Baba,
Sunanda and Akshay,
Dwarkanath Sanzgiri

Contents

Foreword

The term 'sport' stands for dedication, persistence, and most importantly – passion. It is this passion that inspires a person to persevere in the fruition of their dreams. A sport without passion is the same as a man without a heart. Cricket is one such sport with a legion of impassioned followers. The sport fires up the hearts of the young and the old cricketers alike, and inspires the spectators, who have honoured it with their devoted following. Cricket is the real Indian dream factory. Fortunes are made, stories are written.

One such story is that of Virat Kohli, the man who has become the throbbing heart of this long-lived sport. He began swinging the bat at an early age, and rose through the ranks because of his zeal and unique style of playing the sport. His style, whether it pertains to batting or his personality, is much talked about. At the age of twenty-seven, he has already made a mark in sporting history and carved his name upon the minds of many cricket fans.

His name is ubiquitous today, from the front page to the sports page at the end. Often portrayed as a youth icon, even the old legends of cricket see their young selves in him. This story is about Virat, the man of the moment. It seeks to present him from a fresh angle, combined with a rare ability for critical analysis.

There is a profound sense of surety in his work. He is aggressive and domineering on the field. I like this quality and the way in which he exhibits his talent. Few batsmen have been able to engage both the young and the old as this astonishingly committed cricketer. From the moment he takes guard and gets into the business of scoring runs, Virat casts a spell on the audience. His opponents are also known to admire his remarkable ability in playing cricket the way it should be played. He bats on his terms and to me, that is the best feature of his game.

I have seen Virat grow as a cricketer. He possesses the confidence to craft his game under diverse conditions. He has been a brilliant student of the game, dedicated to giving his best and getting the best out of his team. The enthusiasm that he brings to the dressing room is infectious. Very few have the ability to stand out in a team game with such self-assurance and conviction as Virat. A leader with exceptional vision, he can withstand pressure and command the situation with a maturity that is rare.

His rise to the top job in Indian cricket has been well-deserved. The captaincy came with tremendous responsibility and added to his determination to be rated the best batsman in the world. Undoubtedly, Virat is one of the best batsmen in world cricket, given the consistency with which he has scored runs in all formats of the game.

Virat obviously had a great legacy to match up to, with illustrious performers like Sachin Tendulkar and M.S. Dhoni coming before him. However, it is fortuitous for Indian cricket that it has a champion like Virat to carry the team on his shoulders. These are testing times for Indian cricket, and I believe that the team, under Virat's captaincy, is poised to scale unmatched heights and rewrite the history of Indian cricket.

Cricketers have come and gone, but only a handful make their way into our hearts. They make you re-imagine the possibilities of the game and charm you with their astonishing abilities. It is left to us to wonder whether we enjoy only their presence, or see a legend in them, that will become indelibly etched in the history of the game. I can see Virat growing into a legend. He has the potential for becoming a benchmark for future cricketers.

Vijay Lokapally, an eminent cricket journalist and writer with *The Hindu*, has crafted this tale with his eye honed in the game of cricket over the years. I have always admired Lokapally's work, having known him for more than three decades.

In my opinion, he is the right man to tell us the Virat story. Lokapally's credentials as a cricket writer are impeccable and few among the media know the game as well as he does. With an enviable experience of writing on all formats of the game and having toured all the cricketing nations, practically every ground, Lokapally's wealth of cricket wisdom is substantial. He brings to us a story that everyone has been waiting for. A superbly crafted narrative, this book will captivate the mind of the reader with its measured prose and attention to detail.

May 2016   **Ravi Shastri**
Mumbai

Acknowledgements

A call from Gulu Ezekiel, the biggest fan of cricket on this planet and an author of many books on the game, put me on the job of writing the Virat Kohli story. A big thank you to him for getting me this opportunity.

My list begins with Paul Vinay Kumar, the ever-patient and accommodating friend and publisher at Bloomsbury India. He was a great source of encouragement all through the project. I should also thank Rajiv Beri, the Managing Director of Bloomsbury, for having faith in me to deliver the book in quick time.

I can't thank enough two of my best friends from the profession and fine students of the game – R. Kaushik and G. Rajaraman – for making invaluable suggestions and corrections while scanning the manuscript.

Above all K.P. Mohan, the man who taught me the finer points of journalism and continues to do so.

To my editor, Amrapali Saha, for giving shape to my innings with the much-needed technical support. How can I forget Nitika Bakshi (a self-confessed Virat Kohli fan), who kept track of the manuscript submission schedule, and cleaned up and organised the chapters... It was a pleasure working with her.

Support has also come from my wonderful colleagues – Kamesh Srinivasan, Rakesh Rao and Uthra Ganesan. Their infectious enthusiasm has been a huge part of this venture. I hope the book meets the approval of my young colleague, Priyansh R., who is fast developing into a brilliant sports writer, easily the best I have seen in many years.

I owe a lot to India's best cricket writer R. Mohan. My old friends from the profession, G. Viswanath, Manoj Vatsyayana, Ashok Kumat, Debasish Dutta, Sumit Mukherjee, K.V. Prasad, Avdesh Sharma, G.S. Vivek, Norris Pritam, Rajender Sharma, C. Rajshekhar Rao, V.V. Subrahmanyam, Sumit Ghosh and Jaydeep Basu have always encouraged me in my cricket journey.

Rajneesh Gupta has been a constant source of motivation with his kind words and his comprehensive section on statistics is a delight indeed.

My friend from Kolkata – Suman Chattopadhyay – is more than a lensman. He is a treasure house of anecdotes related to the game and the players. Suman has embellished this story with his splendid work.

Finally, I thank every cricketer who I spoke to in compiling this story, especially K.P. Bhaskar, who ought to have played for India. My dear friends, Ghaus Mohammad, Dr Nilesh Mehta, Ziya Us Salam and Y.B. Sarangi, have guided me in this venture, not to forget my genial Sports Editor, K.C. Vijaya Kumar.

Thank you Mukund Padmanabhan, Editor, *The Hindu*, for granting me permission to write this book.

My wife Sunanda and son Akshay deserve the largest credit for this book. They ensured that I met the deadline and did my best to do justice to one of the finest ambassadors of the game in modern times.

Dear reader, over to you....

Vijay Lokapally

Introduction

We hardly saw him in Delhi. He was constantly engaged in outstation cricket matches. Then his appearances became few and far between once he announced his prowess at the national level. Virat Kohli is a talent that grew into a phenomenon, on the strength of his self-confidence that had one constant supporter – his coach Raj Kumar Sharma.

When Virat was making news in Delhi's local circuit, not much attention was paid to his exploits. I had known Raj Kumar from his playing days and it was through him that my interest in this lad grew. His big scores were a consistent part of the circuit that was hugely competitive, since Virat insisted on playing in the company of seniors.

'You have to see this boy,' Raj Kumar would plead. Of course, the junior cricket circuit was agog with raving talk that centred around this immensely gifted batsman. Gradually, Virat's ability to compile big scores with authority unfolded on the national circuit, and suddenly he was catapulted on to the national stage.

Raj Kumar's concern was what if he lost Virat to the sharks of the market. When India under-19 was playing a World Cup final in Colombo in 2006, the team hotel was besieged by agents waiting to sign up the players with prospective commercial value. Raj Kumar wanted to protect Virat from these market forces. Not that he doubted his pupil's commitment, but the boy was too young. Distractions were possible. To his delight, they did not exist in Virat's dictionary. 'You will not get damaging reports about me,' Virat had assured his coach, and he stuck to his promise.

Delhi cricket has produced a stream of gifted players who found their way to the top through sheer hard work and persistence. Raman Lamba, Manoj Prabhakar, Ajay Sharma, Maninder Singh, Atul Wassan and K.P. Bhaskar, were among the early lot of youngsters who had secured their places in a dressing room full of achievers and stalwarts. Virender Sehwag later paved the way for even greater excellence and his contemporaries like Ashish Nehra, Vijay Dahiya, Mithun Manhas, Gautam Gambhir, Amit Bhandari and Rajat Bhatia did the state proud. They left a legacy for ambitious young guns like Shikhar Dhawan, Virat, Ishant Sharma and Unmukt Chand to follow.

That Virat was destined to serve Indian cricket was never doubted by his coach. However, I would be lying if I claimed to have foreseen Virat's growth. The enormity of his talent dawned gradually. It has been a pleasant experience to follow and report on his career, and my privilege to bring this story to you through the eyes and voices of some of his contemporaries and past masters of the game.

Sometimes, his aggression superseded his actual prowess in Delhi circles. I always thought these acts, especially the brazen show of temper, were not a true reflection of the Virat we had known. He was a compulsive competitor, who did not believe in conceding an inch. His dedication was unmatched – spending long hours in the nets under the scorching sun, only to hone a particular shot and work on his technique. He showed early promise that developed into a steely resolve to be the best.

Under the unsparing eye of his coach, Virat learnt to value his cricket. If there was a miniscule deviation from his dictated path, Virat was reprimanded, sometimes harshly with a 'square-cut' on his cheeks, by Raj Kumar. Virat began to look up to Raj Kumar after losing his father, Prem Kohli, at the age of eighteen. The senior Kohli had envisaged his son in India colours, and given Raj Kumar the freedom and responsibility to nurture Virat, who was not even ten when he first walked in to the West Delhi Cricket Academy, with dreams of playing world class cricket.

I have had the privilege of interacting with cricketers from all walks of life – local, domestic and international – and Virat has come across as a determined young man, a consummate batsman of rare elegance, who strove to make his point with the assurance of a champion. He was a champion in his own way. He matched Sehwag in confidence, and never crossed the line, preferring to observe and learn from a distance rather than appear intrusive.

I have seen very few cricketers with the attitude that Virat brings to his cricket. He would not take things lying down – case in point, his verbal spat with Gautam Gambhir during an IPL match. However, he would also never lose an opportunity to show his admiration. Despite his so-called brash behaviour, a confidence boosting trick, I can vouch for Virat's reverence of senior cricketers. His respect for his seniors, his coach, or his family, forms a distinguishing feature of Virat's personality. He was never seen sprawled on the couch in the dressing room whether the seniors were present or not.

Virat does not suffer fools gladly. Even Mansur Ali Khan Pataudi, a player's captain, refused to suffer fools. As captain, Virat has given ample indications of his talent to emerge as one of the greats. He is accommodating, always receptive to suggestions, loves a battle, and takes the onus to excel on himself. There are few like him in contemporary cricket, who put the team first. For those who chided him for being aggressive and demonstrative, his rise in world cricket is a resounding rebuttal. His exuberant celebration after every feat on the field is just a reminder to them that he is here to stay.

He has a wide range of interests, reading does not find a place unfortunately, but he is a powerful brand ambassador of modern cricket. He epitomises the significance of hard work and the benefits of fitness. His diet chart and a punishing fitness schedule are the secrets to his awesome stature in world cricket.

Virat may have seldom played Ranji matches for Delhi, but his heart beats for his state teammates. At every possible opportunity, when visiting home for a short break, you can find him rushing to the Ferozeshah Kotla and cheering his team from the dressing room balcony. He *cannot* stay away from the Kotla if he is in town and Delhi is playing. He never tires of reminding himself the role Delhi cricket had played in shaping his career. He would love to show his gratitude, but for a busy international schedule that takes him away from domestic cricket.

I have seen enormous changes in Virat in the last few years in terms of his attitude towards the game. He has a vision for Indian cricket. He is focused on serving the game in the same spirit that was characteristic of some of the greats in cricket. He worships cricket and the past masters, making every effort to understand its history and give it the exalted position it deserves. Cricket has come a long way from the times of Sunil Gavaskar and Bishan Singh Bedi, when a draw was as good as a victory. Virat symbolises the modern cricketer, a man resolved to win and entertain his audience. He is an icon for a new brand of cricket, positive and intense.

There are few players who are as involved in the game as Virat. His friends say that his energy to assimilate information is boundless. He wants to know everything about everything, and can be found engaged in unending conversations on cars, new business opportunities and discussions on the market.

His passion to acquire knowledge on recent cricketing trends keeps him busy on off days during tours, while his discipline to stay fit is unwavering. Nothing can shake his resolve. Not even his love for samosas and pakoras (deeply fried snacks). He was known to drink Coke all day. Now, he has gladly sacrificed all of that. He eats almonds and grams to maintain a healthy balance in eating, not to forget his fondness for salmon and couscous.

I am not surprised when his contemporaries insist he is 'very respectful' of old relationships. He does not have the airs of a superstar when he runs into cricketers from his junior days. His attention to detail is amazing. We met once after he had returned from a visit to a Nike factory overseas, and he presented a vivid picture of every aspect related to sports equipment manufacturing. He could have set up a venture of his own, based on the information he had managed to gather and imbibe during his short trip.

How Virat has worked on his game is a grand narrative of its own, which he may love to write one day. He is a constantly evolving individual – from an enfant terrible to an enviable role model and a brand ambassador, inspiring the young and the old alike. There were some unfortunate incidents involving him on and off the field, but he was quick to make up and move on. The responsibility of captaincy has worked wonders for him, as he now comes across as a mature leader.

Virat has given us a whole new perspective on batting. He is a technician's marvel and a purist's delight. He can play with fluency in a Twenty20 match, get to a century without hitting a six, play proper cricket shots, and incredibly, as we saw in the 2016 IPL, achieve such a stupendous feat despite an injury in one hand. He batted with multiple stitches on his split left webbing to hit a hundred in a must-win situation against Kings XI Punjab. The stadium, including the opposition, gave him a standing ovation.

His popularity with the youth is unmatched. After Tendulkar, he has emerged as the greatest hit, even with those who do not follow cricket closely. He brings crowds to the Test venues, with children as his most vociferous supporters. He is equally courteous to those younger than him, as well as those much older than him. In the crowd of some cocky and vainglorious dreamers in Indian cricket, Virat stands out as a glowing and unpretentious exception, his batting achievements a testimony to his steadfastness to serve the game with dignity.

He is an ideal player for this generation, cheerful and producing result-oriented cricket. He is also a player for history, having planted the saplings of success that will determine the future of world cricket. Test matches look like they are going to become a thing of the past, but Virat has emerged the possible saviour, an athlete profecient in sprints and also in clearing the obstacles with a gutsy approach. He has a long way to go but knows his course very well, precise and detailed. Virat, with his captivating presence on the cricket field, is a work in progress, and as the recent tour of the West Indies has shown, it is rapid progress, too. Virat the batsman and Virat the captain were on top of their games, the batsman's maiden Test double-ton setting up the captain's third successive Test series victory. Two of them have come overseas, in Sri Lanka last year as India won a series there for the first time since 1993, and now, when India have won more than one Test in a series in the Caribbean for the first time ever. For someone who places great emphasis on individual and team performances away from home, these results would have given Virat great joy, but he will not be satisfied because his pursuit of excellence is relentless.

Let us cherish his gifts to the game of cricket, the classics that he has invented at the crease with the firm assurance of rewriting every feat in the annals of the game. Hail King Virat!!

Prologue

His batting is a masterclass in the art of making runs. He was born to entertain, inspired by a maestro who lit up the world of cricket with his astonishing deeds. Sachin Tendulkar was the god of cricket, worshipped by his fans for enhancing India's image in a game that is a national obsession. Virat Kohli arrived to carry the legacy forward in his inimitable style. Tendulkar was a cricketer's cricketer. So is Virat, a phenomenon who has created a legion of frenzied followers in all formats of the game.

Some of Virat's innings have been hailed as masterpieces. Cricket has not seen a flawless batsman. Not even Don Bradman. Critics always point out the only other country he played in outside Australia was England. We don't know how he would have fared on the tricky spinner-friendly and low-bounce pitches of the sub-continent. He may well have succeeded for his technique was so water-tight, but we can never be sure. Bradman, however, is universally acknowledged as the best batsman ever – tackling the seam and swing in England and the bounce in Australia.

Virat, on his only tour of England in 2014, was a miserable performer, unable to come to terms with the bowlers who snared him on and outside off stump. An abysmal aggregate of 134 runs in ten innings was a sharp contrast to his 992 runs in sixteen visits to the crease in Australia. It set to rest all arguments on his position in the team. He was not short on technique or temperament. Form had deserted him in England. All batsmen, at some stage, suffer from poor form and loss of confidence. To Virat's benefit the phase came early in his career and provided a realistic assessment of his abilities. That he recovered quickly speaks of his potential.

The Delhi boy engaged the attention of the cricket world right from his junior days when he smashed big scores, including double centuries, even before turning nineteen. Coaches were astounded by the punch that he packed into his strokes, mostly on the on-side before transforming into a delightful merchant of off-side shots. He did play across the line often, but he connected the ball firmly in its path and scored runs in abundance to quell any discussion on his technique. As he developed into a compact batsman, Virat's strokeplay assumed a touch of class.

Contemporary international cricket is embellished with sound batsmen like Virat, Joe Root of England, Kane Williamson of New Zealand and South African marvel AB de Villiers. The Virat-de Villiers show in the 2016 Indian Premier League (IPL) was a sight for the cricket gods and a veritable package of batting entertainment. This august foursome has endeavoured to ensure a pristine quality in batting, with Virat leading the pack in his domineering style.

Technique has been of paramount importance in shaping Virat's batting approach. His ability to innovate brings in an element of challenge that keeps his focus in place. It is his focus and tenacity that matter most to Virat. He is game for a battle at all times – ever keen to assume every possible responsibility on the field. The flexibility factor is not an ornamental quality. He often translates it into a compelling performance that can swing a contest on its head. Virat just loves it.

The twirl of the bat that marks his arrival at the crease suggests the man is in a hurry. His gait is rapid and confident – not the swagger of Viv Richards or a pensive amble to the middle of Sunil Gavaskar. They were contrasting images from the past of established masters in their field. Richards was destructive and Gavaskar a firm believer in grinding the opposition session by session. Tendulkar was a combination of both. Virat promises to go beyond with his overwhelming drive to be the best in business.

Virat's strokeplay is stunning. The cover drive is his forte now. Try telling this to those who watched Virat bat in his influential years when he was a compulsive on-side player. He still enjoys the flick and the on-drive, but his strokes to the off have come to assume a majestic touch. The cover drive, whether struck on the rise or inside-out, is a last-moment alteration of his judgement. He self-admittedly loves playing the shot with a flourish and finish that coaches would vouch for as the ideal – right out of the manual. AB de Villiers is a master of this shot, killing the good ball with disdain, and Virat is not far from attaining that standard – picking the length of the ball in a flash and uncorking shots that leave the opposition in a daze.

Virat did not have to be pushed at the training sessions. He would come to the nets with a plan and achieve his short-term goals only to translate them into huge feats during the season. The spark that he showed as a junior has only glowed brightly with time. 'Who would have believed Virat to have travelled this far. He was talented but he has surpassed all expectations. I have been pleasantly surprised,' exclaimed former India speedster Atul Wassan, the man chiefly responsible for drafting Virat into the Delhi team for the Ranji Trophy in 2006. Virat has since figured in just twenty-three first-class matches for Delhi because of his international engagements. Delhi has certainly missed him even as the Indian national team gained from his presence.

Virat began with the image of a flamboyant youngster, now and then coming up with an ostentatious performance, but committed to improving with every step. Little adjustments by Raj Kumar in technique and admonitions when he strayed, ensured he stayed on course. 'I concentrated on keeping the distractions away,' insisted Raj Kumar when reflecting on his pupil's formative years on the dusty cricket fields of Delhi. His student was seen as boorish by the cricket fraternity, but he was a misunderstood young man. Virat was competitive and sometimes crossed the line but there was nothing to stop his rise – from a bubbly youngster to a tattoo-brandishing icon of India's youth. Chants of 'Viraaat, Viraaat' came to replace 'Sachin, Sachin' as Indian cricket underwent a remarkable transformation since the departure of stalwarts like Tendulkar, Sehwag, Rahul Dravid and V.V.S. Laxman.

Virat is the newly-crowned king of Indian cricket. The excitement that marked the arrival of Yuvraj Singh, and the likes of Suresh Raina and Rohit Sharma, has been overtaken by this champion of all formats, putting enormous pressure on him. The expectations when he takes guard often reach the sky because his fans expect the world of him. He knows it and responds by raising the bar every time he serves the team and self. There was a brief phase when he went haywire but hauled himself back into contention. His coach took him into confidence and cautioned him severely to mend his ways and mind his place in Indian cricket. His second coming was an eventful journey since he grasped the lessons from close quarters even as the dressing room lost some of the finest names to have served India.

The stigma of being casual gave way to a man committed to firm up his game. Gifted players like Maninder Singh, Sadanand Viswanath, L. Sivaramakrishnan are prime examples of young talent not living up to their promise and potential. Viswanath's playing career was over at 28 years of age in 1990, two years after he last played an ODI. Maninder quit at 28 too, a year after he played a Test against Zimbabwe at Delhi in 1993. Sivaramakrishnan, who beguiled the best batsmen in business with ridiculous ease, continued till 34, seven years after his last appearance for India. 'They were the most talented cricketers I have known and the biggest under-achievers too,' lamented Kapil Dev, one of the game's greatest all-rounders.

Virat, nearing 28, is steadfastly moving towards attaining an iconic status in world cricket. Past masters have lavished rich encomiums on his fascinating batting and leadership. The bad boy image lies buried under the newly-found persona of possibly the best ambassador for the game. He was described as a cocky youngster, but not anymore. Virat is a mature cricketer with the right balance of aggression. True, he has indulged in some unsavoury episodes, with a fellow cricketer and a journalist, but has quickly learnt the lessons to move on to confirm the impression his coach insists – he is not artificial. He is not the one to allow anyone to take liberties with him.

If Shivaji Park in Mumbai produced some gritty cricketers, the West Delhi culture, with a relentless fight for space and recognition, has contributed towards moulding Virat into a tough individual. The hardships of his early life, the chaos in the bylanes of most of West Delhi, where you get nothing on a platter, meant that Virat was always in battle-gear, waiting to swing his kit over his shoulders and report for the match, riding on a rare confidence that no one can stifle his ambitions. He believed in being combative and has not changed a bit even when competing at the highest level.

Virat hates comparisons. It appears to him as a needless indulgence by the experts and the media to project him as superior and different. That Virat is different is known from his deeds. From the spectacular manner in which he asserts his domain in Tests and other forms of the game is proof of his vast progress. He triggers debates on his stature and it would be a folly to call him a complete player. He knows it too. The critics have the right to delay bestowing that crown on him because he needs to perform in England, play the seam and swing with the same alacrity and perfection he brings to his game when shining on the bouncy pitches of Australia and South Africa. It is apparent that he is very good when the bowlers hit the deck.

What strikes one the most is the way Virat paces his innings. He has learnt to alter his game when the ball swings, stops or seams. He is willing to play the waiting game, allow the ball to hit the bat, instead of going after it. Mohinder Amarnath was a master at leaving the ball. He could do it the whole day. But cricket has changed and batsmen are now appreciated more if they play their shots. A ball should not pass unpunished unless it deserved the respect to be left alone. Virat is adept at altering the direction of the shot at the last moment. He can drive along the ground past cover or smack it inside-out over the fielder. He can also play the straight drive or a cover drive off the same length with a minute shift in footwork and wrists, the grip allowing him to generate that power. Countless times he has played a cover drive or a flick-drive to mid-wicket off the same length. It makes him special indeed.

Modern players have come to laud his aggressive mindset in Tests too, where he is looking to score with authority in front and square of the wicket than nudge the ball behind the stumps. His defence is as compact as that of Root and Williamson, but he scores above them when he falls back on his attacking instincts. He is always pumped up on the field, a deliberate ploy to bring the best from within himself. Off the field, he is calm and an obedient member of the family, absorbing the demands of one and all with a smile.

Virat takes great care to maintain his fitness and of course his body strength that comes from a strict regimen of exercises and diet control. His strength is evident in his shots. He possesses Tendulkar's balance at the crease, holding the bat with a lower grip like the master. Tendulkar's defence was better and Virat has toiled to reach that standard, looking to play with soft hands when confronted with a short ball to see it drop dead at his feet and blunting the spin with superb footwork. He is, however, different from Tendulkar when expressing his freedom of strokeplay. Virat has no fear of failure that sometimes bogged Tendulkar only because of the pressure the nation created.

When Tendulkar or Sehwag got out, the spectators would depart too. Virat does not command that coveted position yet. The contest, however, intensifies or dies depending on Virat's show with the bat. He is working towards attaining his peak as India's Test captain. The chorus to give him the job in the shorter formats too is growing. It is a matter of time when he finds himself saddled with the colossal demands of a cricket-mad nation. The only concern is Virat is yet to face poor time – a bad patch that tests an individual's reslience. Given his ability to adapt and innovate, his cricket may not encounter a dark period in a long time. Indian cricket needs a prosperous and vibrant Virat Kohli.

1

The Early Years

Other than playing an aggressive game, the common thread that runs among Sehwag, Gambhir, Ashish Nehra, Dhawan, Ishant and Virat is that all of them hail from West Delhi, an area in the national capital where the struggle for space and recognition is that much more intense. Lack of opportunities means youngsters have to jostle for a spot in the state squads that sets off a race, which often produces champions. Raman Lamba was a firm believer of this theory. Lamba introduced a trend that has given Delhi cricket a steady stream of international cricketers, with Virat being the most recent example.

The credit for putting Delhi on the national cricket map should go to Bishan Singh Bedi. He led a bunch of ambitious and talented cricketers, namely, Mohinder Amarnath, Madan Lal, Surender Khanna, Kirti Azad to challenge the hegemony of Bombay cricket.

Speaking of West Delhi boys, Sehwag, hailing from a middle-class background, was a role model for youngsters from economically disadvantaged sections who dreamed of making it big. His success story was the outcome of a fierce fight for recognition of his talents. He had little financial support or institutional aid to bank upon, other than the unstinting support from his family. Travelling three hours for a five-minute stint in the 'nets' steeled Sehwag's determination to be counted among cricket's best. When offered a chance to demonstrate his skills in a match, Sehwag left his mark with a brand of cricket that set him apart. His sole aim was to destroy the attack and more often than not, he succeeded in leaving the bowlers embarrassed.

For most youngsters who were inspired by Sehwag, it did not matter if they lacked the best quality equipment. Their sole wish was a level-playing field and when they got one, they delivered the goods. Gambhir was an exception, since his businessman-father could offer the necessary facilities at his disposal. Wassan, supported by a financially sound family, went to Sonnet Club, which was a trusted nursery for spotting and grooming talent among the non-elite in Delhi. However, he was part of a generation of middle-class cricketers – neither pampered nor falling short of going the long distance.

Sonnet Club, under the astute guidance of coach Tarak Sinha, encouraged competition at the club level. It nurtured a series of cricketers who went on to represent the state, as well as the country. When Wassan quit playing, he helped his club mate and a wily off-spinner, Raj Kumar, set up a coaching clinic. They aptly named it West Delhi Cricket Academy (WDCA). It was a happy coincidence that nine-year-old Virat, accompanied by his father Prem, walked up to Raj Kumar on a warm afternoon to learn proper cricket. Eight years later, as chairman of the Delhi senior selection committee, Wassan was to pick the boy for his first Ranji Trophy match in a hotly-contested meeting.

May 30, 1998. This was Virat's first day at the WDCA. Prem Kohli was a lawyer, favourably disposed towards his younger son wanting to pursue cricket as a career. Although no one in the family had envisaged a future related to cricket for Virat, there was no doubt that the lad had set his heart on chasing his passion with due diligence. It was the year when Tendulkar played some of his best cricket. His impressive batting against Australia in Sharjah, during the Coca Cola Cup, had helped him amass a legion of fans for the maestro-in-making, and Virat was one of them. Sachin was the reason why Sehwag played cricket. Sachin would also be the reason why Virat took to the game.

Less than a month after Sachin's exploits in Sharjah, the coaches at the WDCA welcomed this chubby boy. 'He was like most other boys; restless, enthusiastic, keen to get a stint in the nets.

We really hadn't seen anything extraordinary,' recounted Raj Kumar. However, things changed dramatically in a couple of weeks. A few incidents that took place left a favourable impression on the coach. Gradually, he began to discover that Virat was a cut above the rest. What made him realise Virat's potential?

It was a throw. 'I remember vividly. He produced a throw that made heads turn. He was just nine, but the accuracy and power in that throw gave an indication that he had one quality – the feel for the game – and we lost no time in concentrating on Virat,' recalled Raj Kumar. His assistant, Suresh Batra was also stunned by the boy's powerful return from the boundary that had sped like a bullet into the wicketkeeper's gloves.

Within ten days of reporting at the WDCA, Virat was drafted into the playing XI for an under-14 match at the Springdales School. His coaches were astonished by a six flicked to midwicket, which confirmed Virat's remarkable talent. 'We were playing against Playmakers Academy, and it was a matting pitch. This boy casually picked the ball off his legs, and sent it soaring over midwicket. For someone who was not even ten, it was a tremendous shot to play,' said Batra. That match convinced Raj Kumar and Batra that this was a naturally gifted youngster waiting to be honed properly.

Sachin had also demonstrated such phenomenal talent when he had gone through the grind at

Shivaji Park in Mumbai, under the direction of Ramakant Achrekar. Among the first to arrive for nets day after day, Sachin would be the last to leave the training ground in Dadar, a largely middle-class locality in India's commercial capital. Sachin had to fight for a place – on the bus, aboard the local train, in a coaching clinic, and the local league.

So did Virat, born on 5 November 1988, to Saroj and Prem Kohli. The Delhi boy's challenge was to retain his focus and not to lose heart due to the nepotism and favouritism prevalent in junior cricket selections. He was almost close to being lost to the world of cricket because of the shenanigans of the Delhi and District Cricket Association (DDCA). The DDCA, firmly ensconced at the Ferozeshah Kotla, is notorious for its ways of functioning.

Unable to make an under-14 selection, which Virat missed for non-cricketing reasons, further fuelled his ambitions. Virat was anxious to make his mark as a player at the junior level. The selection would have been Virat's first step to achieving his goal, the first step towards playing representative cricket, and to take stock of opportunities for playing at big venues. He was relentless in the pursuit of his goal. No news had come of the team selection. In fact, the meeting at the DDCA seemed to have been highly contentious. It was well past midnight when the team was finalised for a match to be played the following day. Batra's phone rang at two in the morning. His heart missed a beat. A phone call at that late hour would obviously cause concern. Virat was on the other end, wanting to know his fate. The boy had missed the boat, not because of a lack of merit but for considerations other than cricket.

It took tremendous effort on the part of the coaches to console and convince Virat that all was not lost. His father was anxious. There had been offers made to him to move Virat to an influential club in order to ensure his selection. But Prem Kohli was confident that his son would overcome the appalling system rife with nepotism. Eventually, Virat would find his path just like a river that carves its route around obstacles. For how long could the DDCA have kept him down? Finally, Virat forced his way into the under-15 team the following season.

At the WDCA, Virat was easily the best talent on display by a long shot. 'He oozed talent. It was so difficult to keep him quiet. He was a natural in whatever he did and I was most impressed with his attitude. He was ready to bat at any spot, and I had to literally push him home after the training sessions. He just wouldn't leave,' remembered Raj Kumar, his mentor and guide. There was not a moment when Virat would sit idle. 'He had a bat or a ball in his hand at all times, and never wasted his time with the rest. I don't remember Virat coming to the nets late. He would report even when he was indisposed. It was impossible to keep him away from the academy,' added Raj Kumar.

Of course, there were plenty of occasions when he was admonished by the coaches. A few times, he received resounding reminders on his cheeks to drive home the importance of preserving his wicket. Virat, like a faithful pupil, absorbed those moments as part of his learning process. He never repeated a mistake.

It may surprise his fans today but Virat, according to his coaches, was a shy and unassuming student at the WDCA. 'He never raised his voice at any fellow trainee and his eyes only reflected reverence and obeisance,' said Batra. What separated Virat from the rest was his keenness to imbibe the lessons offered to him. 'He was inquisitive. It was not easy to convince him because he had so many questions and supplementary queries. Sometimes I would just fold my hands and ask him to spare me his unending quest for cricket knowledge. His grasping power was beyond his age,' revealed Raj Kumar.

His attentive nature at the WDCA worked well for Virat. He was amazingly focussed. 'We started the academy at the Savier Convent and moved to St. Sophia's School (in Paschim Vihar). His father was the driving force behind Virat's obsession with cricket, but elder brother Vikas and sister Bhavna also played their part in supporting the naughty youngster's journey to wearing the India cap. He was initially making steady progress, and then outstripped the others by a long margin,' said Raj Kumar.

One under-15 match in a local tournament remains unforgettable for Batra. It was held at Picnic Hut, in the Ashok Vihar area of North Delhi. Virat was twelve years old. The lad stunned his coaches and the opposition with a sparkling century. 'It was sparkling because the opponents saw stars during the day. He played some outstanding shots, the power and timing belonging to a higher class. We were convinced that day that this boy was going to make an impact in the world of cricket. Everyone present at the ground left in a trance after the Virat show,' said Batra.

Virat would not miss a match. His father drove him to far-flung venues on his two-wheeler and made sure the zeal to play cricket never ebbed. Virat was a diamond in the rough only for a short period of time. As he learned his lessons fast and integrated them into his game, Virat grew into an effective batsman. Sometimes, he surprised observers with his excellent combination of timing and power. His range of shots was developed on the strength of his strong self-belief. He played the pull and the drive with rare flourish, and came to be respected by the bowlers in the local circuit.

Raj Kumar did not have to worry about the abilities of Virat. 'He was fearless. He trained hard at the nets and took on the senior bowlers like a veteran.' At the first opportunity, Virat would look to pull the ball. There was fire in his stroke play. Training on matting pitches ensured he was quick to respond to the bounce and tame the ball with a rock-steady defence, or smash it with disdain. His shot selection was developed on the basis of his long nets sessions at the WDCA.

Virat's footwork was limited in the initial stages. With success in junior cricket, it improved to an extent where he began playing the cover-drive with a long stride. Even Sachin's stride, when playing the cover-drive, was short. But Virat loved to drive the ball, and the flick was a stroke he had mastered at a young age. He would whip the ball with tremendous power that came from his wrists, along with a sensational timing of the ball. The square cut, Raj Kumar revealed, was not one of Virat's assets, but he added it to his repertoire late in the junior grade. His balance at the crease was undoubtedly an added quality that enhanced the calibre of his batting even as an under-15 cricketer.

Fitness was an uncompromising part of Virat's training schedule. If he was required to give up some delicacies, so be it. Virat was unsparing when it came to following a strict diet, and worked hard on his endurance and stamina. This ultimately helped him become the splendid runner between the wickets that he is today. The foundation was already strong for Virat to build on his cricket dreams. He had nursed a secret desire to go in for tennis, but cricket was the way forward because Raj Kumar kept him under a tight leash.

2

Making a Mark in Junior Cricket

Having missed the selection the first time, Virat worked furiously to force his way into the side. He was the most talked about young talent in Delhi, but the state selectors were not convinced. They were not sure if he was ready for stiffer challenges at the zonal level. However, nothing could have been more preposterous. The mandarins at the Ferozeshah Kotla took time to discover Virat's potential. Once his coach managed to swing their opinion, thanks to his dogged persistence, there was no stopping Virat as he prepared himself to chase his dreams.

His journey began in 2002 at the modest Luhnu Cricket Ground, in Bilaspur district of Himachal Pradesh, with a Polly Umrigar Trophy match against the host. He batted fifty-nine balls and scored fifteen runs. He was obviously disappointed. Delhi umpire Devendra Sharma officiated in that game, with R.P. Singh, and had fond memories to share. 'I can recall a few rousing drives that he played on the on-side. He was the most enthusiastic player among both the teams, and there was a touch of brilliance in what he did at the crease. Even the style with which he asked for the guard displayed maturity. In later years, I saw him grow, and I must say he has learned his lessons well. I don't remember much about others, but I can recall that he was the most busy and involved player on the field. It was a matting pitch amidst lovely environs. He got a few balls on the pad, but it was understandable. He appeared confident though.'

No wonder, Virat was the only one from that under-15 match to go on to play first-class cricket.

Sharma had many opportunities in later years of officiating in matches featuring Virat. 'His batting improved at a rapid pace. He added power to his shots, and some of the shots that he played at that age took one's breath away. His behaviour on and off the field was exemplary. I was once standing in a trial match, and I remember Virat walking up to me with a request. He sought my permission to leave the field because he had some pressing function at home. Honestly, he did not need the umpire's permission because it was just a friendly match. But it reflected his cricket grooming. Credit goes to his coaches.'

Virat's next outing was a precursor to his match temperament. The Palam ground in Delhi was the venue, and Virat, barely fourteen years old, found himself as the target of a boisterous Punjab bunch that had done its homework. 'We knew he was the guy to go after. We had heard about his ability to bat long, and the idea was to put him under pressure the moment he came to bat,' remembered Siddhartha Sharma, now a cricket scribe for a national newspaper and an avid follower of Virat's progress.

Any other youngster would have been rattled by the verbal assault from the Punjab close-in fielders, not Virat. 'He appeared to be the least perturbed. We realised soon that we could not break this boy. He was just going to cement his position to bat for longer. I remember his on-side play was top class, and he showed no signs of gifting his wicket to us under pressure. He had looked like a player of limited abilities, but his progress since then has been phenomenal,' noted Siddhartha. Virat batted 194 balls for his 41 before offering a catch at gully off seamer Bharat Lumba. When the teams met next, in the Vijay Merchant Trophy at the same ground in November 2004, Lumba slammed a century batting at number nine.

Virat's first half-century in a national competition came at the Ferozeshah Kotla, when he cracked a 70 against Haryana in the next Umrigar Trophy match. One of his teammates was Ruushill Bhaskar, whose father – K.P. Bhaskar – was a stylish first-class batsman for Delhi.

Virat ended his first season for Delhi under-15 on a disappointing note with scores of 37 and seven against Jammu and Kashmir. 'He had learned the lesson of putting a value on his wicket, and had promised to improve,' said Raj Kumar.

The 2003-04 season opened on a bright note for Virat. He was appointed the under-15 captain. He celebrated the occasion with a knock of 54, as Delhi scored an innings win over Himachal Pradesh. Ruushill too had a fruitful outing, as he responded with an innings of 70. Ruushill felt confident with someone like Virat as captain. It was clear that captaincy, even at that young age, was bringing out the best in Virat. The next match, against Jammu and Kashmir, earned him his maiden first-class century in a BCCI-conducted tournament. His 119 formed the basis of another innings victory. Arun Bhardwaj, a respected umpire and coach with the Sports Authority of India, was a prime-seat witness to that innings. 'I always look for technique when analysing a youngster and Virat gave me little reason to complain. He built his innings superbly and I came back home wondering if I had seen a future India batsman. If memory serves me right, there was hardly an appeal made against him. I had been told about this lad by some local umpires, and I saw him in action first-hand that day,' said Bhardwaj, the umpire of that match along with Rajan Seth, who also endorsed his partner's views. 'He looked like a special talent,' added Seth.

The match against Punjab in Patiala was much-awaited. This was the most fiercely contested fight in the north, much like the Bombay-Maharashtra rivalry in the west, Bengal-Bihar battles in the east, and the Tamil Nadu-Karnataka fixtures in the south. For Delhi, losing to Punjab was unpardonable – even at the under-15 level. It was the last year in under-15s for Virat and Ruushill. Having excelled against Himachal Pradesh and Jammu and Kashmir, it was natural for Virat to be charged up to take on Punjab. Punjab won the toss and posted a total tally of 399. For Virat, it was a challenge that would prove to be a test for his leadership. However, failure came his way. He was out for five and sank into his seat in the dressing room. Tears flowed down his chubby cheeks, as he refused to reconcile himself to the fact that he had failed when it would have mattered the most to succeed. 'It showed how much he valued his wicket, and self-pride drove him to shoulder the blame. It was rare for Virat not to perform. And here, he just wouldn't spare himself for not dominating Punjab,' said Ruushill.

The process of evolving into a tactical competitor had already begun, as Virat produced one more century – 117 against Haryana at the Tau Devi Lal Stadium in Gurgaon. He followed it up with a 95 in the second innings in a drawn match. For Kamal Juneja, former Uttar Pradesh batsman and a first-class umpire, it was a revelation that he recalled with pride. 'I had seen Virat at the Cambridge School (Rajouri Garden) where I was the coach. He would come with Raj Kumar and his coach would not stop raving about this boy from Paschim Vihar. Virat was a compulsive on-side player, and I vividly remember having him trapped at midwicket by one of my club's best bowlers. The next time, however, he came prepared, and made a mockery of our plans. Talking about that knock at Tau Devi Lal stadium, I must say he was so fluent, so sure, and so positive. He wanted to win and that was the thing I remember most about him,' said the 66-year-old Juneja.

Virat learnt a harsh lesson in cricket etiquette on a visit to Patiala during his first year in the under-17 league. It would prove to be a crucial phase in Virat's journey of evolving into a batsman to watch out for. Raj Kumar had put in a polite word to Chaudhary to look after his ward. The two coaches had played together and there was little for Virat to worry. He was not the captain, but he backed himself to find his way in the junior league. He was already a star, having performed in the under-15 league the preceding year. However, the star was soon brought down to earth by Chaudhary.

'On the eve of the match before the practice, I noticed Virat relaxing on the field, arms crossed behind his head and lying on his back, surveying the others. He was behaving like a star. I announced the squad of twelve and did not name him in the list. Obviously, he was shocked. In the evening, I got a call from Raj Kumar. He sounded worried because Virat had informed him about not getting selected. I assured Raj Kumar that this was just to send the boy a strong message. I felt for Virat because we all knew his immense potential, and I was just making sure he realized his talent and responsibility. I told him you have been rested because you want to relax on the field. I picked him for the XI next morning, but he did not fare well in that match,' Chaudhary said. Virat scored 18 and 21, as Delhi followed-on and scraped through to avoid defeat. Virat was determined to come back stronger in the next match after this poor show.

In fact, Virat arrived with this knock – a 420-ball essay worth an unbeaten 251 – at the Indira Gandhi Stadium in Una. Himachal Pradesh had compiled 366, and Delhi was two wickets down for zero. Chaudhary was worried about the possibility of Delhi conceding the first innings lead, but Virat walked up to him and calmed down the coach. 'He said he would get us the lead. I was impressed with his confidence, and all of us settled down to watch a fantastic exhibition of controlled aggression. He displayed a wide range of shots, and especially won our hearts when he jumped out to the bowlers and hit them through cover. He played like a leader, and gave a glimpse of his temperament by playing his shots along the ground. He was hardly tired in that double century show,' Chaudhary said in praise of Virat's performance on the field.

Looking back, Bhardwaj's assessment of that knock was, 'Virat was composed throughout the match, and this was a sign of a fine batsman in the making. He was rarely perturbed in the innings that I saw from up close, and I was most impressed with his phenomenal match temperament. When Raj Kumar first brought him to me, I had said he would certainly play first-class cricket and the rest depended on his application. Virat had this ability to assert himself, the hunger to score, and the desire to succeed. I could see he was not going to compromise on hard work, and it was evident during that innings at Una. He used to be an introvert, but it was his bat that spoke for him. His tenacity was visible in his beautifully constructed double century. Seeing his game-sense, I was convinced I had made a wrong assessment of the lad previously. He was going to play more than just the Ranji Trophy, and I am so happy to note that I have been proved correct the second time.'

Virat did not fire in the next match against Haryana, but a 179 against Jammu and Kashmir at the Harbax Singh Stadium in Delhi was further proof of his brilliant form. The season had ended on a rousing note for Virat. He eagerly awaited his promotion to the under-19 league. He was rewarded the next year with a match against Haryana, in the under-19 one-day league. Hence, it was time to sing his swan song for the under-17 league before moving on.

He began with a bang – 227 against Punjab. 'A pity I was not there to watch him destroy the Punjab attack. I could visualise his radiant face on making such a strong statement after burying the opposition,' said Ruushill, who had now shifted his allegiance to Haryana. Virat's modest scores against Himachal Pradesh, Jammu and Kashmir, and Haryana, earned him a reprimand from his coaches. However, it was clear that he had reserved his best for the knockout stage.

Uttar Pradesh was given the stick at Eden Gardens when Virat crafted 120 off 291 balls against an incisive attack, which included Bhuvneshwar Kumar, who would become his trusted colleague in the India team many years on. Bhuvneshwar accounted for six Delhi batsmen, but his effort came to nought against a determined Virat. The quarter-final victory pitted Delhi against Baroda, and gave Virat an opportunity to come up with a little gem of batsmanship on demand.

Baroda played to its strength of batting and challenged Delhi with a total of 332. It was a decent score on the Eden pitch. Chaudhary spoke to Virat, who was not the captain yet more than the captain. The team looked up to him. He promised the coach he would finish the job. And finish it he did in style – a 324-ball knock of 228. The Baroda bowlers did not get the slimmest chance, and Delhi was on its way to the final against Mumbai, to be played at the Jadavpur University ground. Virat contributed a first-innings half-century, as Delhi emerged champion with a five-wicket victory. The Delhi dressing room acknowledged Virat's consistent performances in shaping the title-triumph as his association with under-17 cricket came to an end on a glorious note.

It is during this phase that Virat earned a nickname – *Chikoo* (sapodilla). Why would anyone be called a *Chikoo*? Especially Virat of all people, a furiously competitive youngster, rarely sweet to his opponents and not at all soft as the fruit he was named after. Virat was one of the toughest individuals in the team and did not believe in conceding an inch.

Here's the story behind the strange nickname. The Delhi team was playing a Ranji Trophy match in Mumbai. Virat had not even played a total of ten first-class matches. He was part of a set-up that included players he had looked up to – Sehwag, Gambhir, Bhatia and Manhas. He was more than happy to be sharing the dressing room with them.

One evening, he returned to the hotel with his hair nicely cropped. He had spotted a fancy hair salon close by and given himself a new look. 'How is it?' he asked excitedly, as he ran into a couple of younger colleagues. 'Not bad, you look like a *Chikoo*,' joked Ajit Chowdhary, the assistant coach, watching him from a distance.

The name stuck. *Chikoo*. His friends in the team called him *Chikoo*. Virat did not mind at all. 'He was still trying to find his feet in the big world of the domestic cricket circuit. He liked it when he got attention. I have not known a more competitive youngster. He was just hungry for more – runs and attention,' said Chowdhary, perhaps the only person other than Raj Kumar to have admonished Virat.

The world of under-19 cricket beckoned Virat. He was just a step away from a slot in the national team. The responsibility of captaining the India under-19 team, for the World Cup at Kuala Lumpur, was just the shot that he had needed.

In a development that boosted the image of Indian cricket, Ajitesh Argal was declared the Man of the Match at the Kinrara Academy Oval, Kuala Lumpur, as India won the ICC Under-19 World Cup. Argal bowled medium-pace and hailed from Baroda. It was a warm hug from skipper Virat Kohli that made his day, as his teammates cheered for him.

Virat, his goal clearly established, was destined to play in the big league and set new benchmarks. On the other hand, Argal got to play a sum total of ten first-class matches in the next seven years. The difference between their career charts highlights the precocious talent that Virat possessed, when compared to some of his contemporaries in that age group.

India had first won the under-19 world title in 2000, under Mohammad Kaif's captaincy. Maintaining an unbeaten record in the tournament, India had tamed host Sri Lanka in the final, with Yuvraj Singh crowned the Player of the Series. Graeme Smith (South Africa), Michael Clarke (Australia), Mitchell Johnson (Australia), Shane Watson (Australia) and Brendon McCullum (New Zealand), were some of the players who figured in this tournament and went on to make a mark in world cricket in the coming years.

In 2006, India, comprising Rohit Sharma, Ravindra Jadeja and Cheteshwar Pujara among others, made it to the final, again in Sri Lanka, but lost to Pakistan. David Warner (Australia) and Sunil Narine (West Indies) made their mark in the tournament. India won the next two editions in 2008 and 2012, the last one under Unmukt Chand, who struck an unbeaten 111 in the final against Australia. India's consistency saw the team make it to the 2016 final in Dhaka, but West Indies had the last laugh.

Even as the Indian juniors were winning the final in Kuala Lumpur, the senior team, led by M.S. Dhoni, drew motivation from the up and coming players and clinched the Commonwealth Bank Series in Australia two days after Virat lifted the Cup. A thrilled Virat dedicated the win to his late father. He told the AFP, 'He always wanted me to do something big for India, and I am sure this would have made him proud.'

At the end of the final, Virat shared the triumph with the rest of the team. 'It was a great effort by the whole team. I would particularly like to thank our coach (Dav Whatmore), who has been a great support system for us and taught us to believe in ourselves. I feel absolutely wonderful, I am happy, and I do not have words, we believed in ourselves and played as a unit. Marvellous effort by South Africa, a dream final, and thank you team South Africa.'

Virat's elevation as captain of the under-19 was the culmination of a process that had been set into motion by his coach. The target was to make an impact through the ranks, and reap the most from the junior circuit where a youngster learns his lessons the hard way. Failures are fraught with the danger of losing one's place, and comebacks become tough in the face of intense competition. Virat had concentrated on building on his good form, and made the most of it to cushion his bad patches.

Ahead of leaving for Kuala Lumpur, Virat promised himself the title and gave Raj Kumar reason to look forward to his ward returning with the trophy. Once the team secured its place in the final, Virat requested Raj Kumar to fly down to Kuala Lumpur. The coach understood the significance of Virat's plea and rushed to the Malaysian capital. His presence meant the world to Virat. 'It was a big event and he needed my support. I just told him a few positive things,' said Raj Kumar.

Virat was confidence personified at the junior World Cup. In a promotional ICC video, he gave ample indications of his self-belief. 'I am Virat Kohli, right-hand middle-order batsman and right-arm quick bowler. My favourite cricketer is Herchelle Gibbs.' His choice of Gibbs was bewildering since Gibbs had done little of note to command such compliments. In the three years from 2005, Gibbs had had only one Test century to his name. Yet he was Virat's 'favourite' cricketer. But what his coach loved the most was Virat describing himself as a 'quick bowler'. Virat had hardly ever bowled with the new ball and shown any interest to become a fast bowler. But then it was impossible to keep Virat away from action and this was one such example of the captain assuming the role with such confidence. The same Virat bowled off-spin at the 2016 T20 World Cup and even got a wicket off the first ball.

There was an interesting first-ball reward involving Virat in 2011 and Abhishek Mukherjee ably described it on Cricketcountry.com. England, chasing 170 to win in a T20 match at Old Trafford, 'raced to fifty-eight for one in six overs when Munaf Patel struck: Craig Kieswetter hit the slower ball straight to Suresh Raina at cover. Eoin Morgan and Kevin Pietersen saw off the rest of the over quietly; England needed 110 from 78 balls when Dhoni threw the ball to Virat—perhaps the most famous of cricketers who had modelled his action on Chris Harris (well, at least it looked like it). Virat had not bowled before. He did not bowl a proper delivery first up, either. It was a wide down leg. Was it intentional? One could never tell. Whatever it was, it had found Pietersen outside the crease, and Dhoni, despite having a terrible summer behind the stumps until then, whipped the bails off in a flash. Kohli had started his Twenty20 International bowling career with a wide. His career figures read 0.0-0-0-1 at this stage.'

The Kuala Lumpur triumph was built on a strong sense of self-belief among the players. The eleven who figured in the final, went on to play first-class cricket – Taruvar Kohli, Shreevats Goswami, Virat, Tanmay Srivastava, Saurabh Tiwary, Manish Pandey, Ravindra Jadeja, Iqbal Abdullah, Pradeep Sangwan, Siddharth Kaul and Argal.

The final at Kuala Lumpur was interrupted by rain, and the Duckworth-Lewis rule was brought into play which saw India win by 12 runs. India lost five of the six tosses, but not the drive to win. As Kaul recalled, 'Virat was astonishingly aggressive and focussed. He hated losing. He simply talked about winning the final, and sometimes it would lead me to wonder if there was anything other than cricket that engaged his attention. Believe me, some of his planning looked so mature that we would be worried thinking about how to meet his demands. But he was so understanding and brilliant when it came to backing his players. He does not lose his cool if a bowler goes for runs at crucial stages. I have gained a lot from his encouragement. He was a perfect captain to have at that formative stage of my career, and most of the people in the team believed he was set to achieve a lot at the senior level.' The team did perform in the way that Virat had asked them to do, 'Let us play as a nation. Play the best game of your life.'

India won its matches against Papua New Guinea, South Africa, West Indies, England and New Zealand, on route to claiming the title. A century against the West Indies – 100 off 74 balls – brought him accolades. His aggregate for the tournament was 235, but it was his captaincy that caught the attention of most. 'I would treasure my hundred against the West Indies,' he was to comment later. However, one of the highlights of his stay at Kaula Lumpur was a visit to an orphanage that underlined the compassion he had for the under-privileged. 'At all such events there should be such outings with children. It gives happiness to the children. We enjoyed playing with them.' Virat in the years to come would associate himself with such heart-warming ventures, sometimes as part of the senior team.

It was a wonderful culmination for Virat who had played twenty-eight under-19 ODIs and twelve under-19 Tests from 2006 to 2008. These competitions helped him become well-prepared for the senior league, and gave him an insight into the playing conditions overseas. He was rarely troubled by poor form in junior cricket. Virat has always acknowledged the well-planned tours that the Indian Board had chalked out for the young cricketers.

Virat and his boys were accorded a heroes' welcome on their return. A chartered flight brought the team to Bangalore where an open bus parade greeted the players. Among those who received the team was Board of Control for Cricket in India (BCCI) president, Sharad Pawar, who had taken a personal interest in organising the arrangements, as well as in announcing a purse of fifteen lakh rupees to each member of the team.

Virat made a huge impression with his short speech at the function organised by the Karnataka State Cricket Association. 'We had faith in ourselves in lifting the cup. We have played as a team.' The most memorable words for the young India team came from former India captain Rahul Dravid. He called it a 'phenomenal achievement' and went on to glorify their performance. 'What you give us is hope. We can believe that the future of Indian cricket is bright, and I hope that you'll be part of a World Cup win someday. That should really be your goal and inspiration. I just want you to remember that of the boys who won the U-19 World Cup in 2000, only one member (Yuvraj Singh) was part of the (CB Series) winning team in Brisbane. It's something for you to think about. I played for the U-19s in 1991, and was the only one in my team to go on to play for India. This is the start of a critical phase in your lives. What you do from here on is what matters.' Dravid must have been pleased that Tiwary, Pandey and Jadeja did wear the India colours, while Sangwan and Kaul came close too.

The under-19 experience went a long way in constructing Virat's overall development as a cricketer. He remembered what Raj Kumar had drilled into his mind, 'Treat every match as the career-deciding match.' For Virat, playing cricket was his first priority in life. From the moment he rose from his bed, to the time he returned to it, cricket was the only driving force. On the ground, he would not spend one idle moment. Once he took over as captain, he motivated the rest of his team, especially the aggressive brand of players. Virat had always believed that playing cricket on the offensive was the way forward.

At seventeen, he was touring Pakistan and grasping the importance of consistency. Scores of 63 and 28 gave him joy, as India beat Pakistan by 271 runs at Rawalpindi. India also won the next match by an innings and 240 runs, as Virat came up with a strokeful 83 in that victory. India went on to win the ODI series with Virat cracking a morale-boosting 80 in the last encounter at Lahore.

Tours to Malaysia, Sri Lanka, England, New Zealand and Australia, provided Virat the opportunity to test his potential on a variety of pitches. A tri-series in Malaysia in 2007 did not quite give him a stage to perform. He could only bat once in five matches, and score a single run against England, but he absorbed a lot. A century on the 2007 tour in New Zealand saw him grow enormously during the course of a knock of 113 at Lincoln. India drew the Test series 1-1. Within a month, Virat accompanied the under-19 team to Sri Lanka where he experienced moderate success. He participated in a tri-series in the island nation five months later, but went without a fifty in five matches. He came back strongly in the bilateral series against Sri Lanka, with scores off 144 at Colombo and 94 not out at Kandy. He had finally begun to enjoy his ability to bat for longer.

His contemporaries remember Virat constantly engaged in learning his lessons and making mental notes. He backed himself to dominate and dominate he did. He was a player on a mission, a junior cricketer with a rare understanding of the game. He was always a step ahead of the rest because he took his cricket seriously. Most of his questions revolved around how the seniors approached the game, how they prepared, how much they practiced, and dealt with failures. Virat always had a complete roster of questions and would not be satisfied until he was given the right answers. Then again there would always be more questions the next day.

It was a critical phase in his career. He had to excel in his last year in the under-19 squad, even though he had already made his first-class debut and left an impact with that knock against Karnataka at Kotla. The national junior selectors had marked him for bigger roles and their only concern was his aggressive behaviour on the field. Often, it was seen that Virat would seek to confront the opposition, not always winning the battle. However, his involvement in the game was complete and that is what set him apart. He wanted to compete and win. As Kaul had remarked, 'Virat hated losing.'

The 2008 Emerging Players Tournament in Australia gave Virat's campaign a much-needed impetus. He was now under the scrutiny of the national selectors, entrusted with the task of selecting batsmen with the potential to graduate to the senior rank. Along with Virat, those who found favour with the selectors were Dhawan, S. Badrinath, Manoj Tiwary and Abhishek Nayar, considered as the strongest contenders for the team colours.

South Africa, New Zealand and Australia, completed the line-up for the tournament. New Zealand Emerging Players won the final against the Australian Institute of Sports in

Brisbane by three wickets. Virat's best had come against the Kiwis when he hit an unbeaten 120 as an opener in the seven-wicket victory. David Warner of Australia (371 runs) and Dhawan (334 runs) topped the batting charts, with Virat at the ninth spot with an aggregate of 204 runs.

Virat was now ready to step into the big league and the opportunity came soon when he boarded the flight to Colombo with the senior Indian team for a five-match ODI series. It was the beginning of his tryst with world class cricket.

3

Boy to Man

There was turmoil in Delhi cricket. Some seniors were in the firing line of the state selectors as quite a few youngsters were waiting to break into the squad. There was discontent among the seniors. They felt their services to the team were being undermined, but the selectors insisted they had a job at hand – to give Delhi cricket a push in the right direction. The last Ranji Trophy title had come home in 1992, when Delhi dashed Tamil Nadu's dreams in the final at the Ferozeshah Kotla. The pressure was on the seniors and the message was loud and clear – perform or make way for the youngsters.

Vijay Dahiya, a Test wicketkeeper and a stalwart in the dressing room, was given a tough choice – announce retirement or face the axe. He chose to leave on his own terms, paving the way for Punit Bisht to assume the wicketkeeper's role. 'It is always better to go out on a high. I don't wish to block a youngster's way and it is the best time to leave. I don't want to be unfair to Punit. He must get the backing to settle into his job,' Dahiya had said. Dahiya's debut had come against Punjab in 1993-94. He had been a member of the North Zone teams, which won the Duleep and Deodhar Trophy in 1999-2000. He had played in two Tests and nineteen ODIs.

This was not the best time for Virat to take the plunge into first-class cricket, but it was hardly his call. He had made enough waves to earn a place in the state senior team, and was keen to take the first step towards his ultimate goal of turning out in the India colours. Virat was over the moon when he was asked to report for the nets. It was in preparation for the Ranji Trophy season's opening league match against Tamil Nadu at the Kotla. There was another debutant in that game – fast bowler Ishant – who was destined to play international cricket alongside Virat.

Virat's first-class debut (23-26 November 2006) went unnoticed. On a placid pitch, M. Vijay, also playing his first first-class match, and S. Badrinath, his India mates in later years, helped Tamil Nadu make 347, which Delhi overhauled with ease through the centuries from Rajat Bhatia, Dahiya and Dhawan. Virat was caught behind for ten by Vikram Mani off Yo Mahesh. Interestingly, Mani made 52, in spite of a broken finger. However, Mani, in a bizarre case of Indian cricket's selection inconsistencies, never played again and is now reportedly settled in Auroville Ashram.

Yo Mahesh recalls the dismissal vividly. He will always be known as the bowler to take Virat's wicket for the first time in first-class cricket. 'It was a ball that straightened after pitching and took the edge,' said Mahesh. 'I had bowled to him a lot in junior cricket, in the nets, and always found him to be an aggressive batsman. He had a wide range of strokes even in junior cricket and his self-belief was amazing. He would announce and go out and win the match single-handed. I am not surprised to see Virat grow in stature and become the most feared batsman in world cricket.'

The next game, against Uttar Pradesh, saw Virat fall eight short of a half-century. Nevertheless, he made an impression. 'I remember his footwork. There was a certainty in his movements at the crease, and I liked his urgency to dominate. He played his shots and played them fearlessly,' said Rizwan Shamshad, a reputed batsman on the domestic circuit and a key member of the Uttar Pradesh team. Virat was now feeling comfortable with his cricket, and was happy to be a part of the Delhi dressing room. His dreams were slowly becoming a reality.

It helped when Delhi played its third match too at Kotla. Ishant grabbed the limelight with his maiden five-wicket haul as Delhi rocked Baroda, with Mayank Tehlan shining with the bat. Tehlan had started his cricket career with a debut score of 176 against Maharashtra in December 2005, slamming 200 in his seventh first-class match.

However, he failed to live up to his promise, while Virat, whose contribution was a modest 21 in that match, learnt a few important lessons that resulted in Delhi soon getting a young batting powerhouse.

Virat was on the edge now. Three matches had passed without a fifty to his name. His coaches counselled him rigorously. On his own, the boy had made up his mind to cement his place during his next visit to the crease. The opponent was formidable – former Ranji Trophy champion Karnataka. But Virat was prepared. The first day was spent on the field as Karnataka piled up 299 for three with Robin Uthappa cracking an unbeaten 161. Uthappa failed to add to his score the next day, but Karnataka took a firm grip by posting 446. They reduced Delhi to 103 for five, with Virat (40) and Bisht (28) occupying the crease, both raw to the challenge. Virat went home tired. His world would change that night as Prem Kohli passed away due to a cerebral attack on 19 December 2006.

His father was no more and Virat was inconsolable. His mentor, guide, and friend, was gone. From now on, he would have to continue on a solitary fight – take on the harsh world where talent was seldom the password for success. Not that Virat was dependent on extraneous factors, but he was rudderless on that dark night at home. The sombre atmosphere in the house prepared him to be more responsible and disciplined in his quest for cricketing glory.

He waited for dawn. It was winter and the wait stretched to a point where he became distressed. His family was concerned. The teenager needed a distraction to overcome the grief. The family resolved that he had to resume his innings. Virat took the decisive step when he called Raj Kumar. The coach was in Sydney with the WDCA team, and was distraught upon hearing the sad development in Virat's life. 'I remembered his father bringing him to me with a request: I am leaving him in your care and you will be a coach and father figure for my son. I was speechless when Virat asked for my advice that early morning,' said Raj Kumar.

Given the precarious situation in which Delhi found itself, 103 for five, Virat was presented with a challenge that would test his mettle. 'I discussed the team's situation and promised to call him back,' recounted Raj Kumar. It was a tough decision to make, but Raj Kumar was firm. He knew what Virat had to do. 'Go and bat. The team needs you,' Raj Kumar advised the grieving Virat.

For Virat, it was a way of paying tribute to his father who had always supported his ambitions to be a cricketer. The sportsman within gave Virat the courage to face this irreparable personal tragedy, and he was off to the Ferozeshah Kotla to continue with his knock that had halted with the day's play at 40.

Mithun Manhas was leading Delhi, and had become reconciled to the fact that the first innings lead was hard to achieve. 'I normally reach Kotla at 7.45 but I don't know why I was at the stadium gate fifteen minutes earlier than my routine. When I reached the dressing room, I saw Virat sitting (on the bench in the corridor) and holding his head. I was worried,' remembered Manhas.

'What's wrong, *beta*?' asked Manhas. 'I lost my father,' the youngster mumbled.

'I was shocked and honestly did not know how to react,' Manhas recalled. 'This was a situation I had not experienced. There were just the two of us in that corridor, and I looked around for a while to see if I could get someone to help comfort the boy. There was no one.'

Manhas asked Virat to go home, but the latter responded promptly, 'I want to play.' The Delhi captain asked, 'Why? Why do you want to play?'

'Sir, the atmosphere at home is heart-breaking. My family and coach also want me to continue with my innings. They have sent me to play,' Virat told him in a matter-of-fact manner. 'I was stunned by the boy's dedication even in this hour of grief,' said Manhas.

The dressing rooms soon filled up and routine preparations for the day's play began. Word had spread about the tragedy that would irrevocably alter Virat's life. The umpires – P.S. Godbole and M.S.S. Ranawat – took their positions, but not before they had learnt of Virat's personal loss. 'Chetan Chauhan (Delhi coach) had told us about

Virat having lost his father. I felt for the boy and admired his commitment. Delhi was in a difficult position and here was a youngster trying his best to save his side from embarrassment. I knew it was love for cricket that had brought him to the ground. He looked so normal. There were no signs of pressure or grief. I was overwhelmed with emotion when he took the strike. As umpires, we were a bit disturbed, but his attitude to his job was praiseworthy,' said Godbole.

Virat's overnight partner, Bisht, was inspired by his teammate's dedication. 'I was also in my debut season just as Virat, but believe me he looked far more mature. I was speechless when we walked out to bat. Normally, we would have chatted, but this was a very difficult time. He was like a zombie for the initial period. His face was expressionless, and I felt sorry to see a lively character like him look so sad. I did not know how to react and took the best route – bat with him as if nothing had happened.'

A partnership developed. Outside the field, Chauhan simply marvelled at Virat. 'I knew he was immensely gifted and progressing well from the junior ranks, but this side of his personality made me admire him even more. He showed tremendous grit coming to Kotla hours after losing his father. I offered him the option to return home, but he was adamant. I realised that day that this love for the game was going to take him far.'

Tears welled up in Virat's eyes as he went about his job of demolishing the opposition. Bisht was in superb touch at the other end and the runs came fluently. There were admirers of Virat's discipline in the Karnataka camp as well. For coach Venkatesh Prasad, this was exemplary dedication. 'I can only bless him,' he said and put his hand on the young fellow's head. The Karnataka players visited the Delhi dressing room at tea break and offered their condolences. They had never known a player overcoming such monumental grief at home, in order to bring joy to his teammates on the cricket field.

Reflecting on that day, Prasad could not stop talking about what he had discovered at the Kotla. 'I saw a gem of a sportsman. I had been informed at the ground about his father's demise and felt for Virat. But I was shocked when I saw him padded up and ready to bat. I couldn't believe my eyes. His approach was fantastic. It was incredible for a young man, who had just lost his father, to come and take charge. The way he applied himself to the job was outstanding,' recalled Prasad.

For the former India seamer, it was the second time he was watching a teammate return to the cricket field from his father's funeral. In 1999, a certain Sachin Tendulkar had shown similar commitment at the World Cup in England. 'It was a very emotional moment. We were not even aware that Sachin had flown back home for the funeral.

The team as a whole was shattered. Our warm-up before the Zimbabwe match was lifeless,' said Prasad. India's performance against Zimbabwe was lifeless too, as it suffered a loss that shocked its fans. Tendulkar joined the team for the next match against Kenya and came up with a century in Bristol, as a fitting tribute to his late father.

At the Kotla, Virat radiated such confidence at the crease that Bisht was inspired to give his best. 'We did not speak much. In fact, he was lost, and I felt very sad for him. I remember after he played a shot, and I walked up to check if he was doing okay. I mumbled something and just admired him from my end, watching him grow as a cricketer. I had heard a lot about him and was now seeing him up close. His eagerness to make runs was evident from his big scores in junior cricket and here he was demonstrating his art. He was quiet for most of the innings, sticking to normal cricket. There was not one moment when he was hustled into playing a ball,' said Bisht, who made 156, but failed to clinch the first-innings lead for Delhi.

The century was waiting to happen for Virat when he was adjudged caught behind, off B. Akhil, ten runs short of the target. He stood at the crease for a moment, and then began his long walk to the pavilion. He was hurt. Karnakata players should have called him back for he had not touched the ball. Virat had been crestfallen due to the two incidents that had caused him such grief – his father's death and a poor decision. He had already wept at home and now he broke down in the dressing room.

He left the Kotla for the crematorium, even as his team battled Karnataka. For Bisht, it was a day of mixed feelings due to the joy of his maiden century, and the pain of Virat's personal loss. In the evening, as he reflected on the day, his phone rang. 'Congrats for the century,' said the voice on the other end. Bisht was overwhelmed. It was Virat. He had not forgotten to keep track of the match even in his hour of grief. Three days later, Virat travelled with the team to Rajkot to play Saurashtra. He made four and 35 in Delhi's innings defeat. The Ranji Trophy season was over for Virat and Delhi, but he had taken firm steps towards an eventful journey. The boy had grown into a man on that fateful day at the Kotla.

4

The Teachers' Day Gift

September 5 is celebrated as Teachers' Day in India to mark the birthday of Dr. Sarvepalli Radhakrishnan, former President of India, and a renowned philosopher and statesman. The *guru-shishya* (master-pupil) tradition is an ancient one in India and still practised in some corners of the country. For Raj Kumar, his understanding of the importance of Teachers' Day had always come from his son Aviral and daughter Suhani narrating their experiences from the events at school. Until one morning in 2014, the Teachers' Day became unforgettable for Raj Kumar, thanks to someone very dear to him.

'I answered the bell and found Vikas (Kohli) at the door,' said Raj Kumar. Raj Kumar knew that Virat was away in the United States for a photo shoot with a sponsor. Hence, his brother's arrival at his house so early in the day was cause for concern. Vikas too had nurtured cricketing dreams, but could not proceed beyond club cricket. 'I made no distinction between the brothers but Virat was miles ahead,' said Raj Kumar.

Vikas stepped into the house, dialled a number and handed his cell phone to Raj Kumar. 'Happy Teachers' Day Sir,' said Virat, even as Vikas thrust something into Raj Kumar's palm – a bunch of keys. Raj Kumar stood perplexed as Vikas requested him to step out of the house. A gleaming Skoda Rapid was parked at the gate – a gift from Virat to his mentor.

'The gift was great but I was floored by the style and the execution. Look at his sentiments. It was this gesture that convinced me of Virat's humility and respect for seniors. It was not merely because he had gifted me the car. It was because of his emotional touch to the process of reminding me how much he treasured our association, and valued the role of a teacher in his life.'

Virat had played the caring pupil to perfection. Quite the way Nehra had with his coach, Tarak Sinha, gifting him a flat. One fine day, Nehra found Sinha missing from the nets at the Sonnet Club and was told that his coach, residing in a rented house, had been served an eviction notice by the landlord. Disturbed by the development, Nehra, within a week, found a new flat and ensured that his coach never had to face the embarrassment of being asked to shift by some landlord.

Virat had also followed in the footsteps of his role model, Tendulkar. The maestro had taken care of his coach, Ramakant Achrekar, by assiduously looking after his needs. Other than gifting him a car, Tendulkar had always been at his *guru's* side in times of distress. Virat's gesture towards his coach comes in the line of that long tradition of respect and love between the *guru* and *shishya*.

Raj Kumar and Virat have cherished their partnership from the time the boy had come to the coach's academy. 'I always had to keep an eye on him because he would quietly walk into the seniors' group and I had to scold him every time he did that. I was worried for Virat since he was not even ten, but the boy had the courage and willpower to compete with players much older than him.'

Virat insisted that he wanted to train with the senior boys. 'I can do better than them,' he would tell his coach, which he did. He did not merely stop at improving his batting by scoring runs by the tons. He developed his skills in every aspect of the game. He just wanted to be involved all the time. It was difficult to keep him away from action. He wanted to bat, bowl, and field in all possible positions. 'I was accused of being partial and promoting Virat, but believe me I only had to sit back and watch his progress and prove many people wrong. He was intent on making his point without causing any unpleasantness. I can vouch for his integrity and the respect he showed to the seniors at the WDCA,' said Raj Kumar.

Raj Kumar vividly remembers the day he saw this chubby lad holding on to the hands of his father. It was the opening day of the registration at the WDCA. He was among the hundreds of youngsters waiting to be admitted. Raj Kumar divided them into two groups – juniors and seniors. Virat was hardly nine and nonchalantly walked towards the group of seniors. 'Hello, hello', Raj Kumar remembers shouting. 'Go there', he guided Virat to the junior group. 'Such was his self-belief that on the first day of the camp he wanted to train with the seniors.'

Raj Kumar discovered quickly that he had exceptional talent in this little champ. One day, Virat walked up to him with a complaint, 'I want to train with the seniors. These junior chaps cannot get me out.' To check whether his anxiety was misplaced, Raj Kumar asked him to pad up for a session with the seniors. 'Believe me,' the coach raved, 'Not even once did he look out of place. He was a picture of confidence and poise among them.'

Virat was adept at accepting challenges. Raj Kumar, in his playing days, was equally competitive, always striving for opportunities to break a partnership, and keen to bowl at batsmen well-set in the game. When Muttiah Muralitharan was in his first season, Raj Kumar, also an off-spinner, was finishing his career with Delhi. The two were yet to meet but Muralitharan would have been delighted to see Raj Kumar bowl the 'doosra' with a flourish. 'My elbow did not exceed the 15-degree bend,' Raj Kumar laughed, as he spoke about his ability to fox the batsmen, referring to the ICC rule on 'doosra'.

Raj Kumar could rotate his wrist, he does it even know, and flummox the batsmen with the one that went the other way. 'I used it sparingly,' he remarked. Raj Kumar, member of the Madan Lal-led Delhi team, which won the Ranji Trophy in March 1989, beating Bengal by an innings and scoring 210 runs at the Ferozeshah Kotla, never missed an opportunity to regale Virat with stories from his playing days. He found his pupil to be an ardent listener, grasping every moment of the engrossing tales that his coach wanted him to absorb.

'There were lessons in those stories. I would tell him about close encounters and tense moments and how we dealt with them. If you see, Virat has this brilliant quality to study the situation and react appropriately. He is adept at reading the opposition and his team's strength and weakness. It is due to his inquisitive nature, as I remember him hammering me with ceaseless questions,' pointed out Raj Kumar.

Virat was born to play cricket. 'And born to lead,' insisted Raj Kumar. From the day he played his first match for the WDCA, Virat appointed himself as the leader. 'He would become captain and call the shots. Even his seniors would marvel at his reading of the game. When the regular bowlers would struggle, he would offer his wicket-taking abilities. Virat would announce that he would get the set-batsman out and believe me he would get him out. I can't forget his first day at the WDCA. That throw from the boundary, flat into the wicketkeeper's gloves, had startled us. Such a powerful arm at nine years of age! But here he was demonstrating all-round abilities and showing leadership skills. He was not even fifteen when he showed skills at captaincy,' said Raj Kumar.

Raj Kumar can also never forget the day when his ward was mocked at by the under-15 state selectors. Raj Kumar had played along a couple of them. He was obviously hurt when they dismissed Virat as just another youngster from the stables of Delhi's club cricket. 'Virat was in tears and I really felt for the boy. He had done everything possible to merit a selection, but Delhi had some very exacting standards and not always cricketing ones,' Raj Kumar lamented.

The crestfallen and exasperated Virat, unable to comprehend the reasons for his exclusion from the state under-15 team, received a warm and encouraging pat from former India captain Bishan Singh Bedi, who happened to be at the Ferozeshah Kotla as coach of the Delhi Ranji Trophy team. It was the first time Raj Kumar had raised his voice at a fellow cricketer and the two state junior selectors responsible for keeping him out were acutely embarrassed when Virat earned selection next year by scoring heavily in the local grade. At one point, Raj Kumar, in a dilemma, had contemplated shifting Virat to another state, but was stopped from making that move by some prudent seniors.

Virat's fervour to make it big did not stop at getting into the state under-15 squad. He now wanted a contract with a bat manufacturer and Raj Kumar had a task at hand. Virat would nag him until one day the coach sent him to BDM, a renowned brand based in Meerut. 'He is too young for a contract. Are you sure he will go the distance?' asked a representative of the company. 'He is a good investment,' Raj Kumar assured the BDM official. 'You sign the boy and I promise you it will be a long and fruitful association,' assured Raj Kumar. 'He stayed with BDM for a while even after playing for India. I am glad he proved my judgment right.'

The biggest challenge for Raj Kumar was to keep Virat calm. He was like a storm looming large on the field and threatening to sweep them all. He was restless even when he excelled because if he got a fifty, Virat would visualise a century as if by right. It was tough to keep Virat glued to his seat. If the opposition got out cheaply, Virat wanted to go in early and finish the game. 'What if I did not get to bat,' was his innocent query to the coach.

Always slotted at No. 4, Virat had this tendency to pad up along with the openers. If he got out, he never took off the pads until the contest was over. He hated losing his wicket and had to be constantly involved, conveying his message by keeping his pads on. Mistakes were always dealt with a firm hand by Raj Kumar. 'I did not simply stop at scolding him. A few hard slaps have sometimes worked well,' said Raj Kumar, who has been more of a father figure than a coach for Virat.

Raj Kumar has had a huge influence on Virat. The making of Virat was a process that also marked Raj Kumar's evolution as a coach. His rapport with Virat was impeccable. 'I can read his mind. He also knows what goes on in my mind. I have set certain benchmarks for him and he meets them. Sometimes they are about hitting centuries or winning matches. We have worked countless hours on technique and temperament, and he has responded beautifully.'

The flick has always been one of his productive shots. He would nonchalantly pick the line early and meet the ball with the firm face of the bat to hit boundaries at will. However, not always to Raj Kumar's liking. 'I honestly did not like Virat playing the flick. There is always an element of risk when you play across the line. I remember scolding him many times. I wanted him to play the shot to mid-on and not from the middle stump. To his credit he worked hard and came to master the shot.'

Ruushill, his Delhi teammate in under-15 and under-17, averred, 'Virat took pride in his flick shot. He absolutely loves it. I remember an under-19 camp where Raj Kumar Sir was the coach. At the end of a video analysis session, we were asked to fill up a form which included our problem areas and list our favourite shot among other things. Raj Kumar Sir had advocated that we need to play with a straight bat; cover drives and on-drives could wait. Virat put down the flick as his favourite shot and told me to play what I liked best and mention that shot. I also wrote the flick and remember Raj Kumar Sir's smile at the end of it.'

The cover drive, Raj Kumar emphasised, was Virat's strength. He did not develop this shot later in his cricket career, as most critics erringly observe. Virat had always loved playing the cover drive, Raj Kumar confirmed, 'He loved it to the extent that he also began getting out to cover drive. I advised him to avoid the shot. Then he developed a liking for sixes and began getting out while playing the shot in the air. That was not Virat's game. Once I had to scold him severely. This incident took place when he was playing for India. I warned him not to attempt to hit a six until he had fifty on the board against his name. I did not want him to play the cut and the sweep because I was keen on him playing the ball close to the body. I had never trained him for the cut and the sweep because I wanted to make sure he did not err in playing those shots when he had other strong ones in his arsenal. He improved dramatically and is now well-versed in all the shots in the book. The idea was to improve his shot-selection,' Raj Kumar said with pride.

'I am really blessed to have him as my guru. I owe my cricket to him. He has always been there in my tough times. His technical inputs helped me develop as a cricketer. He is an ideal teacher,' Virat was quoted in *The Hindu*. 'It is very important. People don't understand that in the long run, you can't do without a mentor. It doesn't help. I don't talk to many people. It helps to open up because you are under constant pressure, and have to discuss things with someone. I only talk to him. He is the only one I fear. Yes, I do get scolded by him but I like it because it keeps me grounded and focussed. He's the best coach one can ever have.'

Raj Kumar is the only go-to man for Virat when things don't work. 'I keep him grounded by constantly reminding him that he has a long way to go. Breaking records is not the best way to evaluate a batsman. He must be confident, but there is always the danger of over-confidence blocking your objectivity. I look to get the best out of him and we both minutely analyse his failures. Now that he is the captain, I keep telling him not to expect from others what easily comes to him. It is not a feasible method to go about the game. Hence, his thinking and approach to the game is so different from the rest.' No doubt about that. It is evident that Virat is not cut from the same cloth as his teammates, thanks to the guidance of a thoroughly professional coach like Raj Kumar, who was bestowed with the Dronacharya Award on the heels of his ward winning the 2016 Test series in West Indies.

5

One-Day Debut and Career

The grind of the summer cricket circuit in Delhi introduces a player to the harsh realities of competitive sport. Reputations are made and marred in conditions best described as unfriendly. The local champions wait to maul the established stars and even stalwarts like Kapil Dev, Ashok Malhotra, N.S. Sidhu, Yashpal Sharma and Manoj Prabhakar have experienced it for years. Virat was groomed in such situations and it helped him shape his game. It trained him to fight tooth and nail. Moreover, nothing has been handed over to him on a silver platter.

Virat's success as a junior cricketer preceded his elevation to the national team. It was a star-studded line up with Gambhir, Yuvraj Singh and Dhoni as the guiding force. Virat was diligent in looking to make his place and clearly, it was not going to be easy. The team was an experimental outfit and the national selectors were engaged in an exercise to raise a potent combination for the World Cup three years away. Virat was aiming to become an integral part of that team.

Was he fast-tracked into the national side? There were apprehensions whether or not Virat would do justice to his potential. Questions were raised about him and if he could command a place in the national eleven on the basis of his show in the junior tournaments. He was twenty and, self-admittedly, ready to launch his career. The national selectors deserved a pat on the back for keeping their faith in this prodigiously gifted batsman, who knew only one way to play cricket – the aggressive way.

K. Srikkanth, the chairman of the national selection committee, must have seen a bit of himself in Virat. Srikkanth was adept at wading into the opposition with daring shots – hitting the Pakistan stalwart Imran Khan behind the bowler's head was one unforgettable example – and never compromising on his natural flair. Srikkanth was a delight at the crease. So was Virat, who insisted upon batting on his own terms. According to Virat, if the ball had to be hit, it had to be hit. Quite the way Viv Richards and Sehwag played their game, hard and precise.

The National selectors, Srikkanth, Yashpal Sharma, Raja Venkat, Surendra Bhave and Narendra Hirwani were unanimous in assessing Virat as a tremendous potential in limited overs cricket. 'He was scoring runs. There were others scoring runs too, but Virat impressed us with his attitude. His body language conveyed his confidence and the zeal to dominate the crease. We had picked Murali Vijay too, but there was no doubt in our mind that Virat was the big one for the future. The way he handled himself on and off the field was exemplary,' said Bhave, with the experience of playing in 97 first-class matches.

The collective view of the selectors was that Virat would take a long time to succeed in Test cricket. 'We had no apprehensions about his abilities. We knew when push came to shove, he would not falter. He had his plans in place and his vision was crafted on the basis of his well-structured game. His temperament was what I marvelled at. Superb,' Bhave raved.

Raja Venkat recalled the Deodhar Trophy held at Baroda (March 2010), which North won under the captaincy of Virat. 'The way he led the team to victory showed that he had the capacity to command respect. The consistency factor was significant in his growth, but I have seen few players with such assurance and self-belief. And look how his batting has evolved from primarily on-side play to off-side. Of late, you can see him execute the sweep and the square cut profitably. It is this innovation that helped Virat grow.'

Known to grab an offer with both hands, Virat was game to opening the innings in his first ODI at Dambullah on 18 August 2008, two years after his first-class debut. 'I was not surprised by his decision to accept the responsibility because the middle-order was packed,' said Raj Kumar. Virat was not oblivious to the fact that he had to force his way into the team and any batting position was welcome. His stints in Delhi cricket had taught him to be battle-ready and this was the stage for him to show his mettle.

The opener's position was new to Virat. He had never opened the innings in any grade of cricket. And here he was, assuming the responsibility on debut. It was baptism by fire. He saw Gambhir getting cleaned up on the second ball, by the wily left-arm seamer Chaminda Vaas. This cricket was different and he was up against a mean bowler. Virat's contribution was a disappointing score of 12, but not before playing his patent flick off Vaas.

Virat buried the failure of the first match that India eventually lost. He came up with a buoyant 35 in the game at the same venue, two days later. He would remember the match for his maiden encounter with the legendary off-spinner, Muttiah Muralitharan. He faced an over from Murali, got five runs including an edged boundary, and made a few mental notes. He would have to earn his runs at this level. He had begun to enjoy his learning process. Having taken guard at No. 2, Virat took the strike in the next three matches and produced scores of 25, 54 and 31, as India pocketed the series 3-2.

His next ODI was to come a year later at the Premadasa Stadium in Colombo, when India beat Sri Lanka in the final of the Compaq Cup. A place in the team for the ICC Champions Trophy in South Africa meant Virat was on the right track. He was rubbing shoulders with Tendulkar and Dravid, and to this young Delhi cricketer, it was an experience to treasure. A brilliant 79 not out against the West Indies at Johannesburg fetched Virat his first Man of the Match in the senior league. It was a low-scoring affair against a mediocre attack, but his game stood out in the eyes of the experts. Here was a batsman who promised to serve Indian cricket in the long-run.

There was no fixed batting slot for Virat, since his place depended on the availability of seniors like Tendulkar, Sehwag and Gambhir. It took thirteen visits to the crease for Virat to secure his first ODI century – 107 on a wintry day at the Eden Gardens – against Sri Lanka in 2009. The Man of the Match award eluded him, but Virat was showered with lavish praise from all quarters. Sehwag was leading the side and India had a stiff target to chase – 316 in fifty overs. The mission was accomplished in 48.1 overs with Gambhir finishing the contest with an unbeaten 150. Sehwag gave the credit to his Delhi colleagues, but emphasised, 'Especially, Kohli has done well. He got fifties in the Champions Trophy and against Sri Lanka in his last game. We all knew he had the talent and it was just a matter of performing at the international level.'

The words worked like magic on Virat's mind. His cricket progressed at a rapid pace and soon established him as an important part of India's campaign. He also became part of the team that came to be developed with the 2011 World Cup in mind. 'This was a crucial phase, even if early, in Virat's career. He had come to realise his responsibility and his focus was clear. To become a reliable member of the team and create match-winning situations,' noted former India Test wicketkeeper Vijay Dahiya.

Four lively centuries had prepared Virat for the biggest stage he was to perform at – the World Cup. India was the co-host with Bangladesh and Sri Lanka, and the event was termed the best World Cup of all times. The preceding edition (2007), in the West Indies, had left the organisers grieving as India made an early exit. But India was well-prepared this time. It was to be the ultimate tribute from a team to the ultimate cricketer – Tendulkar – who was playing his sixth World Cup.

Virat made a sensational World Cup debut ahead of Raina, with a century against Bangladesh. It was the tournament opener and saw Sehwag in cracking form. His 175 inspired Virat, who came up with an unbeaten hundred as India played around with the host. Sehwag made a mockery of the Bangladesh attack and Virat enjoyed it from a vantage position, as the two contributed 203 runs for the third wicket.

For Sehwag, it was a confirmation of his assessment of Virat. 'Whenever we spoke in the middle, we told each other to not throw our wickets away. I still remember the match against Pakistan in the Champions Trophy (at the Centurion, in 2009), he (Virat) was playing well, but he played a shot straight to long-off. Since then he has scored six hundreds. Sometimes a little nudge is enough for some people. He is a quick learner, and a mature batsman,' Sehwag observed. Virat valued his senior's words and never looked back.

A 59 against West Indies was Virat's next best contribution. India stormed into the final after a hard-fought win against Pakistan, at Mohali, in an expectedly high-profile match that saw the two Prime Ministers – Manmohan Singh and Yousuf Raza Gilani – jointly in attendance at the Punjab Cricket Association Stadium. The mood of the occasion was illustrated in the cordial welcome with which fans from across the border were treated by their Indian counterparts. Virat made just nine as India competently defended a total of 260, built essentially on Tendulkar's chancy 85.

The final at the Wankhede Stadium saw Tendulkar living his dream of winning the World Cup, despite a classic century (103 not out) by Sri Lankan veteran Mahela Jayawardene. Much to the chagrin of the Sri Lankans, two knocks – 97 by Gambhir and an unbeaten 91 by Dhoni – set off celebrations across India. The finish, a six over long-on off Nuwan Kulasekara by Dhoni, was an unforgettable moment for the Indian fans in the stands. Some of them had relished similar emotions as teenagers in 1983, when Kapil Dev and his 'boys' made history at Lord's by shocking the West Indies.

'All credit goes to Sachin Tendulkar. We played for him. Beating Australia and Pakistan and now this, it's a dream come true,' exclaimed Gambhir. Virat carried around the maestro on his shoulders. 'This goes out to all the people of India. This is my first World Cup; I can't ask for more. Tendulkar has carried the burden of the nation for twenty-one years. It was time we carried him. Chak de India!' said an exuberant Virat as he revered his idol.

Tendulkar expressed his sentiments, 'I couldn't have asked for anything more than this. Winning the World Cup is the proudest moment of my life. Thanks to my teammates. Without them, nothing would have happened. I couldn't control my tears of joy.'

From the end of the 2011 World Cup to the beginning of the next in 2015 in Australia, Virat figured in ninety-six matches. His aggregate of 4,278 runs, with sixteen centuries, came at an average of 55.55. His astonishing range of shots constituted a fierce assault on Pakistan in the 2012 Asia Cup at Mirpur. Centuries by openers Mohammad Hafeez and Nasir Jamshed gave Pakistan the cushion of 330 runs to defend. This was a formidable task by any standard, but India pulled it off with thirteen balls and six wickets to spare. Virat was the difference between the two teams.

This was a game Virat would love to relive over and over again. He joined Tendulkar at the crease, with the innings a mere two balls old, following Gambhir's dismissal to Mohammad Hafeez's off-spin. They were separated at 133 and then Virat dominated the 172-run second wicket stand with Rohit Sharma to snatch the contest from Pakistan, the team reduced to a helpless state. Left-arm Wahab Riaz, who had rattled India in the 2011 World Cup semi-final with a five for 46 strike, was mauled to the tune of 50 runs in four overs. Virat took seven fours off Riaz and left skipper Misbah-ul-Haq with a 'We didn't have any answers' lament. However, there was some consolation for Pakistan when it went on to claim the Cup with a two-run win over Bangladesh in the final.

Australia became Virat's favourite destination for run-making in all the formats of the game. In the early part of 2015, he trained his guns on his opponents in the World Cup, starting the tournament with a breath-taking century against Pakistan. An overflowing Adelaide Oval was treated to some vintage batting by Virat, packing flamboyance into his innings, the sheer artistry of his performance adding to his popularity among the fans. If there was variable bounce, it was hardly visible when Virat was on strike. His form was the key to India's hopes of retaining the Cup. Virat's response to his innings was in keeping with his form. 'I just look for an opportunity to stand up to their (expectations) because I hate to lose and I play passionately. I like the expectations.'

However, Virat failed to strike the chord that would have pushed India in the desired direction. He failed to get a fifty in the next seven innings of the World Cup and came a cropper in the semi-final against Australia at the Sydney Cricket Ground. Aaron Finch (81) and Steve Smith (105) set the tone for Australia's domination as the home team presented India with an uphill task of 329 to win. Given India's batting strength, a fight ensued. A lot of it depended on a solid start and Virat coming good when it counted the most. Instead, he flopped when he top-edged a bouncer from Mitchell Johnson. Australia strangled India into submission and Dhoni's dreams of retaining the Cup were blown with Virat's cheap dismissal.

Less than a year later, Virat returned to Australia to establish his credentials as the world's premier batsman in fifty-overs cricket with scores of 91, 59, 117, 106 and eight. India lost the five-match series 1-4, but Virat's stupendous feat won him a legion of fans in Australia. No other Indian since Laxman had earned such appreciation in Australia, where the spectators loved a gladiator on the pitch. Virat had ably demonstrated that he was a modern avatar of the ancient Roman warriors.

Ashish Nehra presents Virat with a memento at the end of a local tournament. Virat's coach Raj Kumar Sharma can be seen behind him.

Photo credit: Raj Kumar Sharma

Virender Sehwag's first meeting with Virat, who is introduced by the Delhi under-19 coach Ajit Chaudhary, at a Madras Cricket Club function.

Photo credit: Ajit Chaudhary

Virat is felicitated by the West Delhi Cricket Academy on being appointed captain of the India under-19 for the World Cup at Kuala Lumpur in 2008.

Above: Virat at the WDCA Academy in 2008; and
Below: The Selfie Ambassador of the Indian team.

Photo credit: Raj Kumar Sharma

From the under-19 days.
From left: Shikhar Dhawan, Virat, Geet Vats and Ruushill Bhaskar.
Photo credit: Ruushill Bhaskar

Raj Kumar Sharma with Virat on his return from a tour, as
he prefers training at the WDCA to this day.
Photo credit: Raj Kumar Sharma

Playing the square-cut at Ferozeshah Kotla in the Ranji Trophy match against Karnataka in 2006. This was the day he reported to play after the death of his father.

Photo credit: S. Subramanium / *The Hindu,* Photo Archives

Glenn Maxwell of Australia attempts to calm Virat following his altercation with Aaron Finch during the T20 World Cup match in Chandigarh.

Photo credit: Suman Chattopadhyay / *Sangbad Pratidin*

Virat has a word with Sachin Tendulkar at a nets session at the Ferozeshah Kotla.

Photo credit: Suman Chattopadhyay / *Sangbad Pratidin*

Virat pays tribute to Sachin Tendulkar in the stands after reaching his half century against Pakistan in the T20 World Cup match at the Eden Gardens.

Photo credit: Suman Chattopadhyay / *Sangbad Pratidin*

Sachin Tendulkar looks on as Virat and M.S. Dhoni chat at the end of Sachin's Farewell Test at the Wankhede Stadium in Mumbai in 2013.

Photo credit: Suman Chattopadhyay / *Sangbad Pratidin*

West Bengal Chief Minister Mamta Banerjee and BCCI president late Jagmohan Dalmiya at the Eden Gardens before a Test match. *From left:* Sachin Tendulkar, Virat, Rahul Dravid, M.S. Dhoni, V.V.S. Laxman and Pragyan Ojha.

Photo credit: Suman Chattopadhyay / *Sangbad Pratidin*

6

Ready for Tests

In the present times, Test cricket faces an uncertain future. Most administrators have been trying hard to address this issue of dwindling attendance at Test match venues. It has resulted in the loss of revenue and genuine fears of losing young enthusiasts to the T20 brand. India, Australia and England are the teams that are most likely to attract fans when they play at home or away. However, that situation is changing. Nowadays, an Australia-Pakistan Test at Dubai is marked by empty galleries. The situation is the same for an England-West Indies contest at most stadiums. Test cricket is widely considered an avoidable fixture in world cricket. The administrators are aware of the fact, as well as the players.

In these times of rapid fall and rise in terms of a career, when a player of Virat's calibre emerges to entertain audiences, one can hope that Test matches may get a new life. Virat, Joe Root, Steve Smith and Kane Williamson, bring value to Test cricket with their organised batsmanship. They raise one's hope of keeping the interests of the spectators in the longer format of the game. This quartet has served cricket with some outstanding work at the crease, with Virat looking a notch above the rest.

For all his talent and consistency in limited overs cricket, Virat would have nearly missed a season of Test matches had it not been for Yashpal Sharma, who saw a rare spark in the young cricketer's game. The national selectors met to pick the team for the West Indies tour, even as the country continued to bask in the euphoria of having won the World Cup under Dhoni's leadership. There was talk of Tendulkar calling it a day and the speculation gained prominence when he indicated his unwillingness to tour the West Indies. The master was cherry-picking his assignments now and it set tongues wagging.

The selectors – Srikkanth, Yashpal, Raja Venkat, Bhave and Hirwani – had their task cut out. The focus was to give a break to new faces. There was a large pool to pick from, but the selectors were not in a hurry to change the composition of the team for the sake of it. A Test cap had to be earned. The selectors were also keen on sending a message that no player had the freedom to take his place for granted.

Most members selected themselves, but the smooth progress was halted when they came to discuss the name of Virat. As Raja Venkat confessed, he was not sure if Virat would be successful as a Test batsman. 'He was undoubtedly good in the limited overs format. But Tests? I was not sure. I must tell you the one man who was convinced and backed Virat to excel in Tests was Yashpal. He was steadfast in his faith that Virat had it in him to be a very good Test batsman.'

The question confronting the selectors was simple: Was Virat ready to play Test cricket? 'He was,' emphasised Yashpal. 'It was my firm belief that Virat was the best player to have emerged from the stables of junior cricket for a long time. You don't have to look a second time when a talent like Virat is in front of you.' Yashpal ought to have known since he was among those who had marked Sehwag as a special talent at an under-19 camp in Delhi. 'Viru did not need a second look. Neither did Virat,' said Yashpal.

Yashpal was a gritty cricketer. He could bat, bowl, and keep wickets. His policy, as a captain, and later as coach, was to refrain from dropping a player without giving him a fair deal. 'I felt this pressure when I was playing and I did not wish others to suffer from it. The pressure of performance can sometimes shake your confidence. At one stage, some people were against Dhawan too, but I stood by him because like Virat, he too had a tremendous passion to play cricket,' observed Yashpal, a member of the 1983 World Cup-winning Indian squad.

What convinced Yashpal to argue so vehemently in favour of Virat? He was candid, 'I saw that spark early when he came into international cricket. He may not have possessed the technique that made Sunil Gavaskar such a great batsman, but Virat had the same fighting spirit. I had that spirit when I was young. Virat was not so fit during his formative years, but in the three years preceding his Test selection he had improved dramatically in all departments. Similarly, I was not sound in technique, but I would make it up with hard work to learn and improve. I was fearless. Virat was fearless too. His eyes spat fire when he took guard and that convinced me to back him.'

That selection committee meeting was actually the turning point in Virat's career. Yashpal was able to put his message across clearly. 'I told my colleagues that even if Virat were to fail, age was on his side. If he clicked, he would serve the team for no less than ten years. I know he flopped (in the West Indies), but he came back strongly. On his first Test tour to Australia, he had a century against his name. It came a little late, but certainly in time to create a fantastic career,' said Yashpal.

Having come through the grind, Yashpal had realised it was important to support an individual when help was most required. It was true that Virat was competing for a place in the team, but he had the qualities to take the big step into international cricket. Yashpal offered a glimpse into the past when he had cheered up a dejected Dravid. Dravid had been facing a hard time. Runs had deserted him and his previous six visits to the crease had fetched him dismal scores of 11, 11, 0, 3, 3 and 4. 'He was leading the side but looked lost, standing in the slips. I noticed he was alone among the crowd. It was a different Dravid. I took permission from the team management to speak to him. When I went to see him in the room, he was sitting on the bed with the bat in hand. I asked Dravid how we could help bring back the smile on his face. He laughed aloud. We did not talk cricket, just general discussions. We went to Mohali next. He hit a century (against England in 2008).'

Virat was a fast learner as Yashpal confirmed it. 'He constantly works on his weaknesses.' When he made his debut in the West Indies, it was obvious that he was overwhelmed. The responsibility weighed heavily on him when he faced his first ball in Test cricket at Kingston. The pitch had some cracks and was expected to assist the fast bowlers. The Sabina Park brought back some bitter memories from a 1976 encounter when Clive Lloyd ordered his fast bowlers to fell the Indian batsmen. If they were dismissed in the process, no harm was done. Skipper Bishan Singh Bedi, worried about the safety of his players – Gavaskar would later term it as barbarism in his autobiography *Sunny Days* – decided not to continue the innings since five of the batsmen were absent due to injuries. The innings was termed as completed. This was the lowest point in India-West Indies cricketing relations.

A lot had changed since then, and India was well-equipped in 2011 to face any short-pitched barrage from the West Indies. India, with three debutants – Virat, Abhinav Mukund and Praveen Kumar – was 64 for three when Virat walked out to join Dravid. He calmly defended Bishoo's five deliveries before scoring his first runs in a Test match – a boundary off Fidel Edwards. He was to fall to Edwards in the bowler's next over. It was a forgettable Test debut for Virat because Edwards had him for 15 in the second innings. India won the Test and Virat had plenty for introspection.

Virat was not well prepared for the battle. He failed in his second Test, scoring zero and 27 at Bridgetown, while a decent 30 gave him some relief at Roseau. His place in Tests had not been secured and that was on his mind as he prepared for the series at home against the same opponent. This was after losing his place in the eleven for the four Tests in England. It was an embarrassing series for India as it lost 0-4 despite the presence of accomplished batsmen like Tendulkar, Laxman, Sehwag, Dravid and Dhoni. The margin of defeats in all matches was staggering – by 196 runs at Lord's, by 319 runs at Trent Bridge, by an innings and 242 runs at Edgbaston, and an innings and 8 runs at Oval. Not since the disgraceful summer of 1974 had India fared so poorly in England. Dravid's outstanding batting was the saving grace as he crafted three centuries, two of them as opener. No other Indian batsman had a hundred against his name.

The transition period for Indian cricket had begun. Although Tendulkar had decided to carry on, the critics began to question his wisdom. He may not have looked a burden on the team, but he was now a mere shadow of his supreme stature as the world's premier batsman. Notably, his next forty visits to the crease in a Test failed to fetch him a hundred. His fans waited for the master to achieve the rare distinction of hundred international centuries, a feat unparalleled by anyone in the game of cricket. At the end of that England tour, Tendulkar was one short of that magical figure, which ultimately came in the Asia Cup match against Bangladesh at Dhaka on 16 March 2012. He was to play one more match – against Pakistan in the same tournament – before ending his one-day career.

All this was happening while Tendulkar's silent admirer, Virat, soaked in every detail of his idol's cricket life. After all, he had toiled hard to be in such a privileged position – sharing the dressing room and living his dream of competing in the big league with the big players. Virat played seventeen Tests with Tendulkar – four overseas, and all of them in Australia. He did not waste any opportunity to learn from the maestro. Tendulkar also took a liking to Virat. Right through his career, Tendulkar encouraged the young guns and he was never short of words in evaluating Virat's ability to dominate.

Tendulkar lavished his praise on Virat when he told a magazine, 'It's a joy to watch Virat bat. His strength is to be able to analyse the situation and adjust his game accordingly. His match awareness is terrific. To be able to have the vision for what the game would look like after four overs or six overs is commendable. He is able to calculate the required run-rate during chases very well. Sometimes his over-aggression might affect him. That is going to happen with aggressive players. That is also his strength. There might be occasions where he will go back to the dressing room and say, "I shouldn't have done it".'

Comparisons with Tendulkar always irked Virat. He responded candidly to set the comparison debate to rest. 'Honestly, I feel embarrassed. It is unfair. Sachin cannot be compared with anyone. Comparisons are not valid from my end. I have looked up to him but I want to be myself while drawing inspiration from him. He is two levels above any player. Sachin was born with talent and I had to work for it. I have been playing well for two years, while he served the nation with grace for twenty-four years. I am inspired by him though I would like to create my own path,' Virat said in an interview to *India Today*.

For all his success in one-dayers, Tendulkar rated Test cricket as the ultimate. He did worry for the future of Test cricket and cautioned the administrators from over-indulgence in the shorter formats of the game. Virat, in contrast, was not unduly concerned about the future of Test cricket. He had worked hard to excel in Tests. He was going to do everything possible to help the longer version of the game retain its appeal.

Virat was with Tendulkar during his agonising moments in the dressing room at the Wankhede Stadium, at the end of his farewell Test against the West Indies. Most eyes at the venue were moist and a teary-eyed Virat walked up to Tendulkar to present him with a thread that he had worn around his wrist. Virat was gifting his idol what he had received from his father as a good luck charm. Virat touched Tendulkar's feet who in turn hugged him. The mantle was quietly passed on that day, from a master to one in the making.

7

Virat Loves Australia

Ian Chappell is a huge fan of Virat. Who is not? The former Australian skipper, a much-respected commentator and analyst, finds little flaws in Virat's batting – his authoritative style, positive vibes at the crease, and a wide range of shots appeal to Chappell. He was a torchbearer of attacking batsmanship in his heyday, a compulsive stroke-player who would not accept the bowler's domination. He believed in batting on his terms, which he did of the highest quality.

Modern cricket has seen some entertainers who have set new benchmarks in aggressive batting. Adam Gilchrist and Matthew Hayden advertised this brand the best, slaying the bowlers in Test cricket with the mindset of a one-day contest. Brian Lara brought poetry into motion in the middle with his silken shots that pierced the field, leaving the opponents dazed. Sehwag transformed the face of batting in Tests, not averse to crack the first ball he faced, getting out at 195 attempting to clear the fence and a few months later hitting a six to reach a triple century, the first by an Indian.

Chappell, and most Australians, admired Sehwag's style. At home, they had Ricky Ponting to showcase the Australian way of batting, always on the prowl to attack. Elsewhere, Chris Gayle had a dedicated following with his astonishing six-hitting abilities. He made no distinction between a Test and a T20 encounter. For him, the ball had to be hit mercilessly and he did it quite often. Dhoni could force the pace of the innings at will and give the match a course that he dictated.

There was some breath-taking entertainment on display when a soft-spoken but determined Laxman walked to the crease and launched a most gracefully distinct genre of batsmanship. He feared no one. The Australians loved it. He played to dominate and the Australians loved him even more for that. Laxman was the darling of Australia on all the four Test tours he made to the sporting nation. He was so popular there that he might have gained an Australian citizenship in a jiffy.

Australia, with its fiercely competitive cricket structure, has always offered the most daunting challenges. 'If you are playing Australia in Australia, you always have to be at your best. There was a time when teams looked forward to do well in the West Indies, but Australia has always proved a hard place to win your cricket battles,' opined Kapil Dev, who took 51 wickets on his three tours to Australia, 25 of them coming on his final visit in 1991-92.

Australia is a benchmark for judging the all-round abilities of a batsman. His preparedness, technique, and temperament, are constantly under scrutiny on the Australian pitches. England offers daunting conditions as well, especially in the first half of the summer when the ball swings and seams prodigiously. However, it is the bounce and pace of Australia that can be unnerving. Dravid, an epitome of correct batsmanship, hit thirty-six centuries in his career and just one in a total of sixteen Tests played in Australia.

Indians have had many memorable performances in Australia. The indomitable Vijay Hazare floored the great Don Bradman with his century in each innings feat (116 and 145) at Adelaide in 1948. He set a high benchmark for others to emulate. Virat had the honour of repeating Hazare's achievement in 2014. It was a pleasant co-incidence that Virat shone at the same venue in an epic Test match that highlighted the significance of five-day cricket in modern times.

Gavaskar, on his first tour to Australia in 1977-78, carved out three brilliant centuries – 113 at Brisbane, 127 at Perth, and 118 at Melbourne. He was six years old in international cricket at that time, and had to establish a strong reputation. He had to demonstrate that he was comfortable even in the most hostile conditions. His record of five centuries in eleven matches on Australian soil has been surpassed by Tendulkar's six in twenty Tests, with that classic 241 not out at Sydney as his best. Even Viv Richards' magnificence fetched him no more than four centuries in twenty-two Tests that he played on five tours to Australia.

In terms of appeal and fan-following, Laxman and Virat have been leaders for different reasons. Laxman won their hearts with his flair and the grandeur that marked his shot-making. Virat played the game just the way the Australians did – in the face, with aggression being the striking element of his approach. Their styles may have differed but Laxman and Virat complemented each other well whenever they batted together.

To begin with, the conditions in Australia are diametrically different from the sub-continent. 'In the sub-continent, the pitches are mostly slow and offer low bounce. When I went to Australia in 1999, I was surprised by the pace and the bounce. You can counter the bounce elsewhere, but in Australia it is steep because the ball climbs from the length itself and not always when the bowler bangs the ball in. It can come from the release and the point of hitting the deck. Very challenging,' felt Laxman, who cracked four centuries in Australia.

The culture of entertaining cricket in Australia invites the stroke-makers to play their best game. Initially, Laxman had been shocked by the aggressive yet positive approach of the Australians.

'They follow this style even in their domestic cricket. Playing to win. Nothing defensive.' Just the way Virat loves to play his cricket – aggressive and always looking to win. It changed gradually as the Australians became versatile in their approach, but did not compromise with their penchant to attack. They would not refrain from setting an attacking field even when the opponents built a partnership.

Virat derived and developed his aggressive instincts from the eight Tests that he played in Australia. The Tests were enough to fuel his ambitions to dominate and convince the young cricketer to spread the message – fight aggression with aggression. He loved it because Australia offers an ideal infrastructure for cricket. Each ground has a distinct character, the spectators are sporting, and they appreciate the game. They also appreciate the opposition even if it ousts the home team, in sharp contrast to the majority of the crowd in India that concentrates on having fun and not so much as understanding the game.

Laxman conceded that the biggest challenge in Australia was judging the length. 'You have little time to make up your mind to judge the length to play your shot. Or not to play your shot. In India, to "a short of good length ball", you can either go back or play it on the front foot. In Australia, the decision has to be quick and decisive, to play or leave the ball. Virat learnt his lessons in good time.'

Virat was excellent at judging the new ball. How to play the new ball has been a perennial challenge for the Indian batsmen before and after Gavaskar shouldered the responsibility with his flawless technique. Dropping the ball dead at his feet, with soft hands, against the meanest of short pitch-loving bowlers was a delightful sight for connoisseurs of technique. Gavaskar did it with style. Laxman and Virat followed in his august footsteps.

Virat was able to negotiate the new ball effectively. The prominent seam of the Kookaburra brand gives the bowlers added advantage, but Virat was adept. Moreover, he was fearless. Once the new ball effect is lost, the Australian bowling becomes easy to handle. 'The first half hour can be very crucial because the ball is hard and judging the pace makes you concentrate all the more. Once you can trust the pace and bounce, you tend to play more shots in Australia than in the sub-continent. Virat picked his lessons very well,' averred Laxman.

Virat's astonishing composure in the face of the storm that was Australia on the cricket field, left a mark on his teammates. He did get a century at Adelaide on his first tour in 2012, but it was the knock at Perth, seventy-five in the second innings, that confirmed Virat's claims as a proficient batsman in the making. He set the process in motion at Perth, in the company of Laxman. Such an experience was of immense help as he scored runs under tremendous pressure, with the likes of Ajinkya Rahane and Rohit Sharma breathing down his neck.

Laxman analysed the Virat of Perth superbly. 'His calmness in the middle and his concentration were very impressive. He closed out all negative thoughts. In terms of technique, he was ready to meet the Aussies with a positive frame of mind.' Virat waited for the ball to come and that was a welcome change from the earlier dismissals at Melbourne and Sydney, when he had wanted to reach for the ball, playing it away from the body and hitting it hard to overcome his anxiety.

At Perth, recalled Laxman, the focus was timing. 'Virat concentrated on timing the ball. I could see he was enjoying this change of approach a lot. He is a natural player and a great timer of the ball. It was a pleasure watching him grow during the course of that knock.' Laxman and Virat batted together in the first innings to add 68 runs for the fifth wicket, which turned out to be the best for that wicket in the match. In the second innings, Laxman did not score, but Virat's 75 was a defining moment. He was the last man out as Australia completed a whopping innings and a 37 runs victory to sweep the series with a 4-0 margin. All the wins of Australia in that series were overwhelming as India faced unprecedented humiliation, smashed in all departments of the game.

Virat corrected his batting formula at Perth. His shots had the required precision since he was confident of placing them. Laxman had made the mistake of reaching out for the ball when he first batted in Australia in 1999 and was quick to advise Virat on this aspect. The batsman stood to gain if he used the pace of the ball on Australian pitches. Virat did precisely that at Perth and his subsequent innings two years later. It was to Virat's advantage that he was a natural back foot player. He did play on the front foot, but using the depth of the crease came in handy on the bouncy surfaces. He was able to transfer his body weight profitably and play the back foot punch, cutting and pulling splendidly. These were shots that would have gladdened Chappell.

Virat carried the confidence of Perth to Adelaide and signed off the series with a century that was scripted under incredible pressure. 'He showed tremendous maturity and confidence to shine in conditions that favoured the bowlers,' remembered Laxman. The knocks at Perth and Adelaide confirmed the belief that he belonged to the big league. He had struggled in the West Indies, against the short-pitched deliveries and appeared in a dilemma – to hit or leave. In international cricket, a batsman can chart a fluent course only if he knows how to play the short-pitched ball. To do that he ought to know his off-stump. However, Virat soon sorted out this issue and had an answer ready for the bouncers that came his way. He demonstrated amply that he was evolving and improving. His repertoire of shots had improved exponentially, but it was his mental toughness and application that made a huge impact on his game. He appeared to have mellowed a bit as he ignored the sledging he was subjected to and did not give it back to the opponents. That Virat was not losing his cool was good news for Indian cricket.

The fact that he had excelled in Australia goes to prove that Virat worked on the technical and mental aspects of his batting. Laxman affirmed, 'He understands the essence of batting under pressure. How to read the situation and the pitch; How to counter pressure; How to bat when chasing or to set up a target; I think the best part of Virat's batting is that he knows how to adapt to different conditions. He has the best mind-set to tackle adversity at the crease and his technique is suited to battle. He is the smartest cricketer on the planet.'

Virat evolved to the extent that he won the hearts of the Aussies when he returned in 2014. The Australians were clueless as Virat amassed runs at will and in a style that was entertaining and compelling to watch. He was in an imperious form – playing the hook and pull – using his feet to open up the field and exploiting the gaps. He had begun to sweep well and that really made Virat a complete batsman. He was not falling prey to the fourth-fifth stump line and was content to let them go. Almost seventy-five per cent of his runs came on the off-side when the bowers tried plugging his liking for the on-side. Virat was adding new shots, especially the reverse sweep that he had come to practise a lot in the nets and later in the Indian Premier League. He was able to read the mind of the bowlers and there was just no stopping him.

Scores of 115 and 141 in the opening Test at Adelaide, when he stood in as captain for Dhoni, were followed by 19 and 1 at Brisbane, and 169 and 54 at Melbourne. He celebrated his elavation and confirmation as Test captain with 147 and 46 at Sydney, at the same time when Dhoni decided to quit Test cricket. Virat matched Australia's positive approach by making a daring attempt to scale the target of 349 at Sydney. That India failed and the match ended in a draw reflected the change in attitude. India was not going to play for a draw under a captain who displayed a strong sense of self-reliance.

Laxman had shown the way with his inimitable class and Virat followed him with an improved batting structure. They shared a quality. 'I always looked for boundaries. Virat is also a boundary hitter,' Laxman affirmed. Virat, soft hands and great wrists, has been a powerhouse on Australian pitches. His first thought is always to hit a boundary. If not, convert ones into twos and twos into threes, thanks to his astounding fitness. It is a pity that Laxman and Virat did not have many opportunities to bat together in Australia. It would have been a symphony for the Aussie ears. They love performers under pressure. Laxman was one. So was Virat.

8

Failure in England

Brash. Arrogant. Undisciplined. An upstart. These were some of the words used to describe Virat. His aggression on the field, looking the opposition in the eye, and his readiness for a confrontation, marked Virat as the man to watch on the field. He worked to gain attention. He enjoyed the scrutiny, right from his formative years in the game that he dearly loved. At no point in his career has Virat shown disrespect to the game or the seniors. However, he is not the one to accept things lying down. 'You give me. I give it back,' is his philosophy, simple and effective.

Tanmay Srivastava, Virat's captain in the India under-19, learned very early that Virat was special. 'We were told that climbing a pole is not that hard as hanging on to it. But Virat climbed and sat on the pole with amazing authority. He bridged the gap between junior and first-class cricket with apparent ease. In junior cricket, you tend to face average bowlers in every team, not in first-class cricket. Virat did not care for reputation. He batted with an aim to make runs and win matches. Failure would make him livid. The greater the pressure, the more he enjoyed. No wonder he matured so quickly to become such a major force in world cricket.'

Virat has been astonishing in his progress. His hunger for runs is legendary. 'He will accumulate runs even on a pitch full of slush. I have not seen a batsman so hungry for runs,' raved Sehwag, himself a scourge of the best bowlers the world over. Sehwag batted as if there was no tomorrow. He never made any claims but asserted his supremacy in a compelling style, dismissing good deliveries and never looking weighed down by the occasion. It was this quality that Virat imbibed from watching Sehwag.

Batsmen from the Western part of India are known to abhor gifting their wickets. Gavaskar, Dilip Vengsarkar, Aunshuman Gaekwad, Ashok Mankad, Dilip Sardesai, Sanjay Manjrekar, to name a few, put immense value on their wicket. Give them a chance and rue for the rest of the match. They hated getting out and it was this quality that greats from the North like Bedi, Kapil Dev and Mohinder Amarnath would advocate their juniors to emulate. For Virat, the lessons were learnt simply and effectively. DO NOT THROW YOUR WICKET. It became ingrained in his mind as he climbed the charts of popularity and stature in Indian cricket.

The North has produced some flamboyant cricketers in the last decade or so, with Sehwag being the torchbearer of stroke-filled batsmanship. The likes of Gambhir and Dhawan convinced Virat the way forward was to look to dominate early and plunder for runs. He did not believe in a stuttered start. Initially, he was a slow starter. 'In North, we love hard-hitting batsmen,' averred Kapil. Virat hit the ball really hard. 'I can't remember Virat checking his shot in our junior cricket days,' recalled Srivastava. That Virat loved to build his innings was proof of his ability to absorb fast. He made notes from watching batsmen who believed in grinding the attack, but jumped at the first opportunity to slay the bowlers.

The brazen behaviour on the field was often an act put on by Virat. He, like many of his contemporaries, was convinced that he had to look aggressive in order to pump up himself. It helped but it also came at a cost. A cheap dismissal would set him off on lengthy introspection and analysis. It is a quality that Gavaskar and Tendulkar shared. His desire to innovate, improve and compete sometimes led to haughtiness in him, especially when the best could not stop him. As noted coach Tarak Sinha observed, 'I have seen him grow steadily. He was one among many in his first few years. And then he became the one to watch out for. I don't remember many youngsters play the ball on the rise as Virat did. You can see he is at such ease when the ball comes on to his bat. The faster it comes, the faster it goes. He has learnt to play the moving ball late. He is not committing to play the ball early anymore and that has happened because he is sure of his footwork and balance. He does not react to the ball and has a big heart. I am reminded of Lamba, who signified the aggression of West Delhi cricketers the best. There are shades of Raman in Virat. He too loves a fight.'

Former Delhi keeper-batsman Devendra Sharma spends his time honing young talent at Delhi's Sonnet Club. He has a keen eye for spotting a good youngster. He was among the few who followed Virat's career since Raj Kumar was also a former Club mate. 'Look at how he has adapted to the challenges of international cricket. He is not a one-dimensional player. In fact, he has no favourite stroke and that speaks for his game. He can play all shots.'

For Virat the ball is meant to be dismissed from the square. It was no different for Sehwag nor for Gilchrist, the effervescent Australia stroke-maker, capable of finishing a contest on his own. A tremendous hand-eye combination allowed Sehwag the freedom to smash the ball because he could pick it early. Virat too spots the ball early but combines the co-ordination with caution. Sehwag would not mind trying to square-cut the incoming ball, but Virat would wait, constantly analysing the situation even if looking to get on with the job without losing time. No wonder he was always most respectful towards Sehwag, who never craved for attention, but did not miss making his presence felt by making as strong a statement as possible.

Any sportsman is pulled up short by failure. Often, such moments are suffered in solitude because sport can be cruel and demanding. In cricket, batting is described as a one-ball experience. True. You can lose your wicket to the first ball. 'You live every ball. Why fret over what comes next. You have to play the ball on merit and if you are prepared, nothing can stop you. Good batsmen don't give their wicket easily and not at all when they realise the good form,' observed Sehwag. This has been Virat's philosophy, to live every ball.

Brian Lara was a master at milking good form. He had once said that he made the best of his good form as a cushion for bad times. Gavaskar, Mohinder and Vengsarkar read the game very well and made adjustments in their batting. When Virat encountered poor form on the 2014 England tour, it was a lesson in the disguise of failure. Obviously, he was not reading the ball well and had technical issues. During good times, he could whip the ball from outside off to midwicket, but England presented a challenge. It was a situation that found Virat mentally unprepared. He was perishing to the swing and had no clue where his off-stump lay. This was an excruciating phase because he was keen to perform in England, which offers the bowlers and batsmen a competitive platform to test their skills. Virat had failed and it hurt him immensely.

Elsewhere, his bottom hand had helped Virat garner runs in style. 'His grip is similar to Zaheer Abbas. There is a gap between the hands when he holds the bat, but it is amazing how he plays the same shot in the air with high elevation or along the ground with a last-moment adjustment. Zaheer used to do that and Virat executes it exceptionally. I know he did not make runs in England, but that was an aberration he can easily overcome when he plays there next. Virat is too good a batsman to repeat the mistakes,' said Yashpal.

Virat's body language on that England tour was not convincing. His scores in ten innings read an appalling 1, 8, 25, 0, 39, 28, 0, 7, 6 and 20. He was brought down to earth firmly and his reputation was dented. He had failed where it had really mattered for him to excel. He was greeted by Stuart Broad, with a beauty at Trent Bridge, the ball ending in the slips after forcing him to play. The same bowler got him the second time and trapped him plumb. Virat's first Test appearance in England was hardly worth remembering. Neither was the second nor the subsequent ones.

India won by 95 runs at Lord's after escaping with a draw in the first Test. The team had played to its potential with Vijay, Rahane, Bhuvneshwar and Ishant in tow. The 7 for 74 spell by Ishant, in England's second innings, gave India the match and a 1-0 lead. The team's good times ended with the Lord's triumph, as England swept the next three Tests. Virat was experiencing a torrid phase. James Anderson had snared him in the first innings with a gem that moved late. On his next visit, Virat was flummoxed by Liam Plunkett's first ball when he shouldered arms. Virat was evidently struggling to decide which ball to play and which to leave. His sad story continued at The Rose Bowl, Southampton, where England won by a whopping 266 runs.

The assertiveness in Virat was missing. It was a meek posture that he presented, unsure of his technique, and struggling to cope with the pressure. The comforting thought was that the team backed him. Once again, he was beaten by Anderson's late movement and off-spinner Moeen Ali lured him with his flight. Nothing was working for Virat even though the two innings at The Rose Bowl had fetched him 67 runs. He was not at his best, evidently looking to come out of the worst period of his career. Disaster lay in store at Old Trafford where India lost by an innings and fifty-four runs. Virat fell to Anderson in both the innings, edging to slip on both the occasions. He was just not able to fathom the rapid slump in form. And luck too. The edges were going to hands. India's rout, and Virat's, was completed at The Oval with England winning by an innings and 244 runs.

Next time, it was not Anderson who tormented Virat. Once again, he decided to leave the ball and was caught in front by Chris Jordan. Same story was repeated in the second innings, but this time Virat played the ball, the intended flick-drive ending in slips. The Test-tour was over for Virat with nothing to show in terms of achievements. The one-day series that followed left him more embarrassed with scores of 0, 40, 1 not out and 13, as India salvaged its reputation with a 3-1 margin after the first ODI at Bristol was abandoned without a ball being bowled due to rain.

'Anderson was extraordinary in that series and Virat not at his best. We were not worried about his calibre. It was a phase that needed to be forgotten,' said former national selector Bhave in Virat's defence. 'Many batsmen have fared poorly in England after shining in other countries. It took a monumental effort from Dravid (in 2011) to drive home the point that top class technique was the most essential ingredient for success in English conditions. Hard hands can cost you dearly in England and it can happen to anyone. Sehwag though proved hard hands can work in Tests too and you can play your shots right away. Virat was on his first tour to England and all the selectors felt that he needed unstinting support. It prepared him well to tackle failures,' said Bhave. India had lost all the four Tests in 2011, but Dravid had given an exceptional account of his skills with centuries at Lord's, Trent Bridge, and The Oval.

When push comes to shove, Virat is always considered the one to execute it best. His temperament was said to be similar to Dravid, who would create a zone for himself, shutting out the negative thoughts and concentrating on the missiles that were hurled at him. Bowlers took pride in taking Dravid's wicket. Similarly, they now angled for Virat's scalp, the most treasured batsman to bag. He fought his way to bury the dark experience of England. As Bhave noted, 'Virat now looks to be on a different plane altogether. He has been in sublime form since that forgettable tour and his consistency has helped Indian cricket grow. I am glad to note that we did not make a mistake by fast-tracking him into Test cricket. He has handled himself excellently.'

Virat matured as a player after that England tour. He was more patient, respectful of the opposition, and learnt to wait for the ball. 'It was an important development in his batting. To wait for the ball,' observed Bhave, who has spent many summers in England playing in the minor leagues. The tour to England was a harsh lesson for Virat. He was to learn quickly and firmly establish his place in the team.

9

Excelling in Tests

Good players always claim that Test cricket is the ultimate stage because it is a test of their endurance and temperament. Endurance and temperament are the two essential qualities that a player has to incorporate into his game, along with the skill factor, if the aim is to excel in the five-day format. Each session throws up new challenges and it becomes increasingly stimulating. For batsmen, the joy of excelling in hostile conditions is an experience to be treasured – a century with the ball seaming and darting around in England, or whizzing past one's ears in Australia, enhances the individual's reputation. To stand up to a barrage of short-pitched bowling and counter it with daring is enough to elevate a batsman to the high pedestal of cricketing glory. Great batsmen have always prided themselves on scoring centuries away from home. Virat's maiden hundred, obviously deeply cherished, came in most testing circumstances, at Adelaide, within a year of his debut.

Virat's innings of 116 proved futile because Australia won but he triumphed as he crafted his first Test century. He was over the moon even as Indian cricket lay in shambles. Australia had closed the tournament on a 4-0 standing and the Indians had no place to hide. There was talk of retirement, as is the case when a team fails. In this case, individuals like Tendulkar, Dravid, Laxman, Sehwag, Dhoni and Gambhir had failed to hit a century in the entire series. Virat was the lone Indian to reach the three-figure mark and that too in the final Test. It was a series no Indian cricket fan would like to remember. Virat was an exception though. The century was a compelling statement of his potential and a confirmation of the fact that he was ready to serve at the highest level.

Double centuries by Ponting and Michael Clarke had already left the Indian bowlers reeling, and then the batsmen led things further down. Virat's century was an act of defiance and a lesson in constructing an innings. It drew admiration from the seniors even as the stand-in captain Sehwag dismissed talk of retirements. He was happy that the talent he had watched from up close in Delhi had arrived on the international stage. His century was a confirmation of his dexterity in making runs. However, what stood out was the dynamism that Virat brought into the Indian camp when he took on the Australians and paid them back in the same coin.

Subjected to constant sledging by the players and taunts from the spectators, Virat decided not to allow the Aussies get their way. 'To give it back verbally and then score a hundred is even better,' he said. 'They sledge when they get frustrated. Obviously it was hot out there. They were constantly sledging so that they could spoil our concentration. They were really having a go at us.' Virat was a run short of his century when he got into a verbal spat with the opposition.

'(Ben) Hilfenhaus said something to me that was quite unnecessary. It was out of the blue. He wasn't even bowling. I had just survived a run-out on 99. He said something to me that I can't obviously say at the press conference. I gave it back to him. Ishant and I came together and got stuck into them and they got really pissed off. I usually play my cricket like that and I like to give it back,' said Virat as the world enjoyed a glimpse of his combative attitude.

Virat also spoke about his issues with the spectators. 'In Sydney, they were after me because I hadn't scored any runs, and today they were angry because I got a hundred. It hasn't changed; only the reason has. It is really, really frustrating at times, they say things which shouldn't be said on a cricket field. If they come here to enjoy a game of cricket, they should do that and not get drunk and abuse cricket players. It's not fair; if the players say anything they're fined and banned,' said Virat, putting the issue of aggression and sledging into a clear perspective.

Virat's first century at home – 103 against New Zealand – was in keeping with his decent form. After an innings win at Hyderabad, where Cheteshwar Pujara hit a century, India came to Bangalore and wrapped up the series with a five-wicket victory. Virat got his second Test century and first Man of the Match honour after Dhoni finished the match with a six. Virat was delighted because he had played a crucial role in guiding the chase with an unbeaten knock of 51. He had stolen the limelight from some of the stalwarts and it augured well for Indian cricket that a young batsman had assumed the responsibility to deliver. 'It was a tricky situation when I went out to bat and MS and I took it ten runs at a time. I needed to be more patient and it worked. There was more turn today, it was a great cricket wicket. I always love this crowd.'

Incidentally, Virat had been confident of India achieving a victory at the end of the third day's play. 'Even earlier on, when people asked which hundred is most special to me, I say the hundred in the Adelaide Test against Australia. I didn't have that feeling ever in my life, before or after— and I felt it again today. When your patience and technique is being tested and you manage to score a hundred, it always pleases a batsman.' He was an important element in the middle order when India scaled the peak of 261 to win.

Within three months of the thumping win against New Zealand, the Indian team faced resistance from England, which had done its homework on competing in the sub-continent. Grass on the pitch at Nagpur had been misconstrued as a surface that had essentially been flat. India played four spinners, but the game ended without a result. For Virat, these are still memories to be cherished. In a match where a bowler (James Anderson) was declared the Man of the Match, there was praise for Virat. His century stood out in the Indian camp even as Dhoni missed his by a run.

He made a realistic self-assessment following his century. 'I was really eager to do well in this series so I probably got a little too desperate to score runs and that is not good for a batsman. You need to be desperate, you need to be hungry, but you can't get too desperate and start putting pressure on yourself. I am really pleased to have got this hundred,' he had remarked.

He was candid in admitting, 'I was waiting for this one innings. I never doubted myself, never thought about what people were saying. I have always believed in my abilities. You can't keep performing in every series or every match, these ups and downs happen, but you need to stay positive and have the same mindset whether you do well, or you don't do well.'

Virat was the toast of the cricket fans and evoked a sensational comment from Gavaskar. 'Till the fourth day of the Nagpur Test, I would have backed Dhoni. Now that Virat has come up with a hundred under trying circumstances, even curbing his natural game, he discovered a good part about himself. He is ready to take on the mantle of Test cricket (captain). That needs to be looked at in a positive manner by everyone concerned, as that is where the future lies,' Gavaskar said, in his show on NDTV. India lost the series 1-2, but Virat matured as a cricketer.

It did not take long for Virat to carve another notable century against Australia. There was much to celebrate about his feat. His 107 at Chennai was timely because it also contributed towards an Indian win. The fans lapped it up. A Virat century. A Dhoni double hundred. It was a triple bonanza for the Indian fans. Once again, Virat assumed a veteran's role by sharing fruitful partnerships with Tendulkar and Dhoni. The Indian captain set an example by walking in at No. 6 to guide the lower half of the innings. The depth in India's batting complemented Virat's efforts for a winning cause. The fact that he was beginning to play a fundamental part in the team's rise and ensuring that the team could bank on him, saw Virat emerge a key player in the scheme of things.

The sporting Virat chose to give his views on Dhoni's innings before talking about his own. 'If he bats like that, you don't need to say much. Coming in after Tendulkar's wicket, we needed a big partnership and he strung in one with me. When in form, he can hit the ball a mile and take the game away from the opposition. Very few people in the world can bat like that. It was very special to watch. For someone who bats, keeps, and captains in all the three formats, he's incredibly fit. Hats off to him for that!' Thereafter, he was brief about his own knock. 'A few people watching me felt it was weird that I didn't perform well against England. I took some time off the game and came back fresh. I was hungry for runs before the series and it helped.'

Next up was a decisive moment in Virat's career. He was to face searing pace in South Africa, and he did not disappoint. His 119 at Johannesburg at the end of 2013 packed in a lot of substance. Doubts had been raised in the run up to the match about Virat's ability to stand up to scorching pace. Dale Styen, Vernon Philander and Morne Morkel came hard at Virat, but he put up a solid front, blunted them in style, and won the Man of the Match award for his excellent batsmanhip. His 96 in the second innings helped India set up a target of 458 runs. South Africa gunned for it, but fell short by eight runs after looking to cruise at one point. The drawn result surprised Virat and he did comment on South Africa giving up the idea of going for the win.

'Absolutely, cricket has won. The way this Test match has been played over the last four days, it was pretty competitive with both teams coming back strongly in one session or the other; it was a fair finish. Everyone was pretty shocked honestly, we didn't think that they would stop going for the score because with eight runs an over and with Philander striking the ball pretty well, and he can bat, we have seen that in the past, I don't know what happened,' said Virat at the end of the match.

His first visit to New Zealand with the senior team was noteworthy for his century at Wellington. The performance in the series helped Virat claim the ninth spot in ICC rankings, the first time he figured in the top ten of the world. His progress had been remarkably sustained and the century in trying conditions at Basin Reserve helped Virat share the limelight with Brendon McCullum, who slammed 302 in the second innings. McCullum's century did not create the winning stage for his team because Virat stood in the way with a strokeful 105 not out. The positive nature of Virat's knock was the biggest gain for India in a series where he aggregated 214 runs in four innings.

Adelaide again beckoned Virat in 2014, this time to produce his best – a century in each innings. Australia set a furious tempo for this Test when David Warner crafted a 163-ball 145 on the opening day. This was a typical Aussie way of launching a contest, but then Virat, the stand-in captain for an injured Dhoni, was not to be found wanting either. He emulated Hazare who had performed a similar feat at the same venue in 1948. Virat acknowledged the help from Tendulkar for the two outstanding knocks of 115 and 141.

'Speaking to Sachin in Mumbai was helpful as far as the mental aspect of the game was concerned, but coming to terms with myself or being at peace with myself is more of a self-realisation. Here, I wasn't thinking about milestones, only about targets. The only thing I kept telling myself was to believe,' he said. 'Just believe in myself. In every ball that I play. The intent was to get a boundary for every ball. That's how I could keep out the good balls. If I was trying to defend already, I am giving the bowler a chance before I play the ball.'

This was also an innings that saw Virat generously employ the sweep shot. He confessed, 'It is probably the first time in my life I've swept so much. Surprisingly, I haven't practiced it that many times. I've been practicing the lap a lot, but not the flat-batted sweep. But it surprisingly started coming off, I don't know how. I saw the ball, put my foot down, tried to sweep and it came off. I was feeling good about it. Mentally, I was feeling positive that I can sweep and that's a big thing with me.'

Virat set new records in the process of demonstrating his prowess to the Aussie spectators. His aggregate of 256 runs was the best by a player in his first Test as captain.

A target of 364 raised prospects of an exciting finish on the last day. It was intriguing too because a 'rough' on the pitch meant that the surface was not ideal for batting. However, Virat told the team that they had to play for a win. He said later, 'At no point, did we think about not chasing down the score. We have come here to play positive cricket. No sort of negativity is welcome in this group. That's the kind of belief we have come here with. This has been one of our strongest performances overseas in the past two-three years, and I am really proud of the way in which the boys played in this game. They showed a lot of heart and character.'

Virat's philosophy of cricket came to the fore when he remarked, 'Wins and losses are part of this game. We didn't play for a draw. We played for a win. We lost. No problem. If we had won, the questions would have been different, the answers would have been different. We have to maintain this kind of an approach if we have to win abroad. If we try to play for a draw, the negative approach creeps in. I'm only hurt because we didn't cross the line when it looked pretty bright for us. But that's the way sport goes, that's the way Test cricket goes.'

However, the Test left a bitter taste in the mouth from the war of words between the rival players. Warner, Dhawan and Virat attracted fines for their poor behaviour.

Virat ensured that Australia had taken notice of his growing stature before the year ended, with a well-constructed 169 at the majestic Melbourne Cricket Ground. This was to become Dhoni's farewell Test and the shocking announcement came at the end of the match. Virat was a regal performer indeed, with support from Rahane, who also cracked a century during their 262-run partnership for the fourth wicket. The Indians had managed to force a draw – a first such result in seventeen years at the MCG. Virat and Rahane justified the faith reposed in them by the think-tank of the team. This pair was considered to be technically and temperamentally adept at handling the pressures of international cricket. The centuries they compiled at the MCG established Virat and Rahane as the pair to depend on in the middle order.

Entrusted with the responsibility of captaincy, Virat stepped into the role in style when India played Australia in the fifth and final Test of the 2014-15 series. Virat's splendid run Down Under culminated in yet another century, his fifth on Australian soil. Australia had posted an imposing 572 and India, riding on Virat's century, responded with 475 on the board. Australia, looking to force a win, presented India with a target of 349 to win. On the victory chase, Virat spoke about the positive approach. 'At a certain stage, I thought we could go after the target. I thought it was worth taking that risk. You can try and see what happens and as the situation developed we pulled off a draw. Sometimes you have to take that risk.'

He had no complaints about his team's approach. 'It is always pleasing to see guys stepping up and going out there and competing in difficult situations in Test cricket. Obviously, the result hasn't gone our way, but we have certainly played the kind of cricket we wanted to. As we gain more composure, and improve in a few areas, you will see us cashing in and actually winning Test matches going to the fifth day.'

India did make a decent attempt, but the game ended in a draw. The match brought down the curtain on an acrimonious series, involving two top teams of contemporary cricket.

The Galle International Stadium offers a serene ambience for cricket, but left-arm spinner Rangana Herath unleashed a storm on the Indian camp, with his flair to take wickets and inflict a defeat. It was an embarrassment for a batting line-up that had claimed proficiency in its handling of slow bowlers. There was abundant purchase for Herath from the pitch and India encountered humiliation in the first of the three-match series in Sri Lanka.

Dhawan and Virat extended their competition at the nets to the middle and their stroke play matched the splendid atmosphere of the ground. However, it was unfortunate that their batting failed to lift the Indian spirits. Herath spun a deadly web and India succumbed to a 63-run defeat. Herath claimed seven wickets in the second innings, after a hundred each in the first innings by Virat and Dhawan had caused concern to the home team. India wasted a lead of 192 runs to leave Virat a dejected man at the presentation ceremony. 'We should have been smarter with how we should have gone about playing the spinners in the second innings. The need of the hour in the second innings was to take calculated risks when you are chasing a small total in the fourth innings. Our intent was lacking. We let the opposition in. It was a case of us not playing fearless cricket – we were tentative,' Virat emphasised. To end on a happy note, India did go on to win the next two Tests and clinch the series, but Virat ended up with bitter memories of the occasion when his eleventh Test century proved futile.

10

The IPL Journey

The Twenty20 format revitalised cricket at a time when big events were being condensed into small packages. Like long-form news encapsulated into blurbs that pop up on newsfeeds. The emphasis was on instant results. A format that was result-oriented was enthusiastically welcomed by young fans of the game. Twenty20 was conceptualised with the aim to win back the young generation, deemed to be lost to football, basketball and tennis. It brought forth a very different kind of youth who believed the best way to play cricket was to play it differently. They were not averse to putting away the coaching manual because of the demands of Twenty20. If truth be told, it worked.

It was a format that produced a new variety of fans. It also created an eclectic cast of cricketers who were happy to pursue their dreams in the shortest format of the game, even as the purists bemoaned the slow death of five-day cricket. This cricket encouraged the genre of robust hitting. There was little room for the faint-hearted because last-over and last-ball finishes became the norm. There was entertainment galore, even for those who did not understand the nuances of the game. It lured spectators from various backgrounds who were happy to treat Twenty20 as a great entertainment package. Although this was a kind of cricket that left the purists exasperated.

The stadiums were packed at T20 games and deserted at most Test venues. The administrators, however, loved it. The success of T20 filled their coffers and it helped them sustain the longer format. Cricket was at a crossroads. It rained sixes at T20 matches. The audience loved and lapped it up. There was hope. A new set of players had emerged to rewrite the rulebook of cricket. It was no longer necessarily played as desired by the coaches. A fresh manual had emerged with the traditionalists wondering if they had any role left to play in the future of the game.

When the idea of a Twenty20 World Cup was mooted by some of the established Test-playing nations, the resistance came from the Indian Board. Stalwarts like Tendulkar and Dravid opted out of the race and the stage was left wide open to the young and untested. They grabbed the opportunities. Young legs on the field brought young admirers in the galleries. Cricket went through a remarkable transformation. A huge rise in female spectators at cricket venues than ever before set a new trend in India, as Dhoni and his team brought home the inaugural Twenty20 World Cup in 2007 by beating Pakistan in a pulsating final at Johannesburg.

The Twenty20 World Cup galvanised the game in the sub-continent. Private leagues, notably the now-defunct Indian Cricket League (ICL), sprung up to celebrate India's triumph and eventually led to the launch of the Indian Premier League (IPL), a brainwave of Lalit Modi, a businessman with a vision to reinvent cricket as an entertainment package. The IPL was actually an offshoot of the ICL that threatened to challenge the official cricket structure. Fearing a parallel league that could undermine its own efforts at promoting the game, the Indian Board banned the ICL. The IPL turned out to be a more than healthy replacement.

Virat followed the fortunes of the Indian team in T20. He entertained hopes of making a mark in the newest form of the game without losing his focus on playing Test cricket. He did not have to wait long as the IPL arrived a season after India's World Cup triumph. Cricket would never again be the same after 2008, when the first edition of the IPL signalled a revolution of sorts.

The inaugural IPL was a resounding hit. A full house at the Chinnaswamy Stadium in Bangalore heralded a new era on 18 April 2008 and any doubts over the future of 20-over cricket were laid to rest. It was an astonishing night. McCullum walked out to open the innings for Kolkata Knight

Riders with Sourav Ganguly, who took strike. He faced eleven more balls before the stage was taken over by McCullum, who swept the opposition with a stunning charge – 158 not out off 73 balls, with ten fours and thirteen sixes. More sixes than fours signified the nature of the game and the changes that batsmen brought to their style.

The administrators appeared mightily relieved at the heavy turnout of cricket lovers. McCullum's knock went a long way in establishing IPL as a successful event in the annual cricket calendar. What more could the spectators have asked for? There was plenty of action, a result to celebrate, and all of it delivered within three and a half hours, the same time one spent watching a movie at a nearby theatre. It hardly mattered which team won because the cricket world was delighted at the outstanding response from the fans of Bangalore. Among those who watched the McCullum show from close quarters was Virat, making an appearance for Royal Challengers Bangalore (RCB). He was to remain loyal to the franchise in the subsequent eight editions.

The IPL, with home and away matches, introduced an element of entertainment to attract spectators to the venue with cheerleading girls and music at the ground enlivening the ambience. The television viewership for the event was heartening too, but the franchises insisted on filling up the stands. The support obviously had to come from the players' fraternity. Good performances on the field were recipes for success and the dazzling start that McCullum gave was what clinched the deal. RCB caved in meekly and Virat managed a poor score of one in his IPL debut, but he gained from playing in and against some of the greats of the game, like Ponting, Dravid and Jacques Kallis.

The best thing about IPL was the opportunity it provided for the youngsters to share space with some of the luminaries of the game. Virat obviously was keen to make the most of it. Virat's first season in IPL was insignificant. In twelve innings, he accumulated a miserable 165 with the highest score being 38, as RCB managed a mere four victories and suffered ten losses. For a high profile team, it was disappointing, but RCB was still learning its early lessons in T20.

A last-ball finish in the final on 1 June 2008 was a blessing for the organisers and a resounding confirmation of IPL's popularity. Chennai Super Kings (CSK) and Rajasthan Royals (RR) were competing for the inaugural IPL crown and the expectations were high in either camp.

A sea of spectators had descended at the DY Patil Stadium in Mumbai. As they stood in a serpentine queue to gain entry, the ticket-holders were fascinated by the sight of Modi, the IPL Commissioner, arriving in a helicopter a few metres from the stadium. This captivating sight showcased the opulance of the event.

CSK posted a target of 164 and RR made a fervent effort, with the equation coming down to eight runs off the last over to be bowled by L Balaji. For RR, a lot depended on the batting skills of Shane Warne and Sohail Tanvir, one of the eleven Pakistan cricketers to figure in the first edition of IPL. Incidentally, Pakistan players were not picked by any of the franchises in the subsequent editions of the IPL because of the November 2008 militant attack on Mumbai. They were part of the 2010 auction, but not one of them found a place in any team.

For Tanvir, it was a memorable tournament. He had destroyed CSK with a 6-for-14 strike at Jaipur when the teams met for the first time. He hit the winning runs in the final, in the company of Warne, who had played the decisive role as player-cum-mentor. The RR celebrations drove home the point that there was no clear favourite in this brand of cricket. The underdog stood an even chance and RR proved it on that glorious night at the DY Patil Stadium. The cricket administrators had found a mantra to keep the game alive. As the purist would lament, the devil of T20 was born with the success of IPL-1.

The IPL caravan travelled to South Africa in 2009, when the Union Government conveyed its inability to provide security to the tournament because of the General Elections. The event was a huge success and firmly established the IPL as one of the best sporting leagues in the world. The format of the tournament remained the same and Virat was part of the RCB squad that lost the final to Deccan Chargers, at Johannesburg, by two runs. Anil Kumble was at his best, with a spell of 4-0-16-4, but RCB failed to accomplish the modest target of 144 as veterans Kallis and Dravid let the team down. Once again, Virat could not come to terms with the game and his aggregate of 246 was not in keeping with his form and reputation. There was a half-century to boost his image, but Virat continued to be a disappointment.

For RCB, the title remained elusive and it finished third in 2010, with a win over Deccan Chargers though Virat progressed as a batsman. His aggregate (307) was better than ever. It was also the first time that Kartik Murali, a wily Test left-arm spinner, was bowling to Virat in the powerplay. 'I got him on the third ball,' recalled Kartik. 'He was looking to drive me over midwicket, but holed out to (Angelo) Mathews in the deep,' said Kartik. The bowler had noticed an anxious Virat aiming to charge down the pitch and was quick to counter him with a clever change of pace to fox the batsman.

'There was something about Virat that struck me from the time I saw him first (in 2006). His urgency to improve stood out. It was as if he wanted to improve with every innings that he played. It did not matter if he was figuring in a five-day match or a T20. He was always looking to develop and dominate,' said Kartik.

Virat was making news when Kartik was turning out for Railways. 'I knew him as a junior cricketer with immense potential. He looked like a kid with amazing talent really. His level of commitment showed that he was a special player. He could play a few shots like no one else. What I don't like is critics comparing him with some of the former greats. Let Virat be Virat. He is not somebody who will rest on his laurels. He has evolved constantly, changed his game and added a variety of shots depending on the situation. He has worked on his batting and you can see how his shots on the off have improved phenomenally. His work ethics can be a model for the young generation. See how he punishes himself. His fitness regime and his diet control. All this has contributed to make Virat what he is,' Kartik opined.

Virat was to come into his own in the 2011 edition with 557 runs to his credit. Four half-centuries justified his form, but it was a pity that he was back in the dugout often when looking good for more. In the final at Chennai, the contest was at the halfway stage when Virat lost his wicket. Eventually, RCB went down to CSK by 58 runs. The top half of the RCB batting had crashed to the CSK spinners and the margin of defeat aptly reflected the difference in the teams. RCB had it in its ranks to win the title but Virat alone could not have proved the decisive force.

For Virat, the next two editions of the IPL coincided with his rise in Indian cricket. He was a regular member of the one-day squad, working his way up in the batting hierarchy for a place in the Test squad. The team had begun to rely on his ability to swing the matches, but the title remained out of reach for RCB. It finished fifth in the league stage in 2012 and 2013, the year when spot-fixing allegations rocked the tournament and threatened its future. Three Rajasthan Royals (RR) players – S. Sreesanth, Ankeet Chavan and Ajit Chandila – were arrested for allegedly fixing games.

The upheavel in Indian cricket left many reputations in tatters. The BCCI president N. Srinivasan had to resign from his post when investigators found his son-in-law, Gurunath Meiyappan, a key official of the CSK, involved in placing bets. He was later banned for life from cricket activities, along with RR co-owner Raj Kundra, who was also found guilty of placing bets. The Supreme Court appointed Justice (Retd) Mukul Mudgal to lead the probe and Gavaskar was asked to head the BCCI to oversee the conduct of the IPL. This was happening even though CSK and RR were allowed to participate in the seventh edition of the tournament, but disqualified for 2016 and 2017.

A seventh place was all that the RCB managed in 2014, when Virat played all the fourteen matches with a top score of 73. RCB showed signs of going the distance in 2015 when Virat was more consistent with the bat – compiling 505 runs in sixteen innings, with a highest score of 82 not out. Losing to CSK in the Qualifier at Ranchi, with a ball to go, left RCB frustrated. The champion's tag remained out of reach for the gifted RCB line-up.

Constant analysis has pushed Virat's game a notch higher every time he has taken guard. As Kartik noted, 'The way he analyses, the way he paces his innings, the way he factors his risks, I think he should have been a brand ambassador for some insurance company. He is not a complete batsman yet. We should wait before coming to that conclusion. He is very good against fast bowling and on certain types of pitches; he can also play spin well. But we must see how he manages on seaming tracks or on raging spinning tracks. Knowing him, he must be working on these aspects I am sure. He always thinks ahead.'

It was his planning that reflected so strongly in Virat leaving the bowlers trembling in his wake, in the ninth edition of the IPL. His presence at the crease gave little chance to the opposition. His commanding form grew enormously as Virat came to make the 2016 edition of the IPL his own. He did not leave any room for mistakes. He led by example and batted with a purpose to lend a touch of invincibility to RCB after a shaky start.

Virat was able to build on his form, fitness and an overall game that allowed him to adapt because he was supremely confident. The wide range of shots gave him the freedom to pick the areas he wanted to explore. The bowlers had no clue since Virat carried the assurance of a batsman who had arrived at the crease with a hundred already against his name. When a batsman relinquishes his fear of failure, he finds himself in a zone where nothing can hurry him into making an early mistake. It was this zone that defined Virat of 2016. He succeeded by playing percentage cricket – reducing the risky shots.

If RCB recovered from six defeats in the first ten matches, it was essentially due to the incomparable AB de Villiers and Virat. They came up with some astounding knocks, even under pressure, and carried their team into the final. The intensity that marked their batting was the standout feature of the tournament that saw Virat at his best. He scored four centuries and seven fifties in sixteen innings for an aggregate of 973 runs. His hundreds came against Kings XI Punjab, Gujarat Lions and Rising Pune Supergiants. He signed off the tournament with a 54 against Sunrisers Hyderabad in the final, with a hope to return next year to fulfill his ambitions of an IPL crown.

11

Virat and One-Day Cricket

At the 2016 ICC WorldTwenty20 semi-final in Mohali, when Virat Kohli demolished the Australian attack, praises poured in for him from every part of the cricketing world. Gavaskar, considered to be one of the finest judges of technical excellence, had the final word when he said, 'At the moment, he's (Virat) got to be the best limited overs batsman in the world. There is no question about it. There is not the slightest doubt about it because he is beyond phenomenal.' That brings us to the question of the best one-day batsman in the world at the moment and Virat may well be the answer.

What was Virat? A Batman? Or a Superman? Could he achieve the unachievable by dominating in all forms of the game? Virat's unbeaten 82 at Mohali saw India give a successful chase for a total of 161 and make it to the semi-finals. He did not score a century in that game because his best was reserved for the crucial tie. 'I was on tenterhooks watching the young genius at play. It was just mind-blowing stuff,' remarked Gavaskar.

The former India great was commenting on Virat's ability to plan his knock during a chase. 'Look at his record especially when India needs runs or is chasing runs. He wins the match for them every single time with his combination of power and timing, going hand in hand. Very few batsmen have this ability to play with both the top and the bottom hand,' Gavaskar said on his TV show. It was T20 cricket, but Virat was the only one putting in consistent performances in the ODI format.

Virat's exceptional prowess as a batsman comes into play best during a chase. Twenty-one out of his twenty-five centuries have come in a winning cause. Out of which, ten of those innings were constructed at home, under exacting conditions due to the low bounce pitches. The low bounce factor becomes a vexing issue when batting in the sub-continent. Incidentally, four of the centuries that led to Virat ending up in the losing camp were in overseas matches.

For Virat, a lone hundred in 2009 was followed up by three centuries in 2010, and four more were added to the tally next year. In terms of productivity, 2012 was his best year with six centuries to his credit and all away from home. He appeased his supporters with three hundreds in 2013, four in 2014, and two each in the next two years with an astonishing sequence of 91, 59, 117, 106 and 8 in January 2016.

Modern cricket presents a variety of challenges to a batsman. They have to be proficient in all formats of the game, while the degree of flexibility determines the character of the individual as a player. Virat was ahead of the rest in determining the chase, which was reflected in his record. Virat's elevation as vice-captain of the Indian team, for the 2012 Asia Cup at Dhaka, was based on his strength to carry the team on his able shoulders. Essentially, it stemmed from his commanding performance at Hobart during a 2012 tri-series match.

It was his ninth ODI century and one with a far-reaching impact on his career. At the end of the Hobart knock against Sri Lanka, Virat had featured in 82 ODIs and scored 3,233 runs. Two days after Virat played this innings, the Indian selectors met at the Cricket Centre in Mumbai to finalise the Asia Cup team. The remark that shaped Virat's bigger role in the team was made by Srikkanth, chairman of the selection committee, while outlining the roadmap for Indian cricket. 'Hats off to Virat Kohli for the way he has played. We have to start looking towards the future. The selection committee and the Board felt Kohli is future captaincy material,' said Srikkanth. By giving him the vice-captain's job, the selectors had confirmed Virat's growing stature in world cricket and put him in the forefront to lead the team once Dhoni relinquished the post.

Former Australia captain and India coach Greg Chappell evaluated Virat's rise fittingly. He wrote in his column in *The Hindu*, 'Just when it looked like the wailing was about to start, Virat Kohli turned in a stunning batting performance of exceptional class that ensured that the tour would not end in ignominy. He is talented and is a fierce competitor. He has given, as well as he has got on the field and he is still standing and delivering at the end of a tough tour. His mettle has been tempered in a hot furnace. India has a player here that can lead the revolution. Kohli could well be the role-model for future Indian cricketers.'

For years, most Indian batsmen had faltered when standing up to the barrage of short-pitched bowling overseas. However, Virat, in Chappell's opinion, belonged to a different breed. 'What has set Kohli apart from many of his teammates is that he has handled the short ball with aplomb. He drives well, has an array of cross-bat shots when challenged with the short balls. He is composed and is rarely trapped with his hands in front of his body to the short ball which allows him to counter-punch. But first, he must address the anger that seems to be at the core of his being,' said Chappell, insightfully.

The Hobart innings was an astounding performance. India was confronted by a gigantic task – to get 321 runs in forty overs in order to earn a bonus point and stay in the tournament.

It would have been tough by any standards, but Sri Lanka had the advantage of defending it with the opposition under severe pressure. That India achieved the target was a tribute to Virat's position in the side as a match-winner. His unbeaten 133 off 86 balls left Sri Lanka battered.

'I decided to give it my all. We took it like two T20 games. That was our plan and we executed it,' said Virat, revealing the tactics at the end of the match. 'At the break, we decided to go for it. We needed a good start in order to chase down that total and get a bonus point. We got a great start and then Gautam (Gambhir) and I were involved in a crucial century stand. It really set the game up for us. We looked to get one boundary in an over and keep taking the singles. If you needed 100 runs in the last ten overs, it was very gettable. We kept wickets in hand. We decided to keep our Power Play in reserve and Sri Lanka not taking their Power Play early really helped.'

Sri Lankan speedster Lasith Malinga, one of the most difficult bowlers to score off, was nevertheless taken to task by Virat. 'He's a very difficult guy to get away with. Once you get the better of him, you make sure it stays that way. They persisted with him even when he gave away 24 runs because they knew he could get them wickets. I was hitting the ball well, he was bringing it in, it is my natural shot,' an excited Virat explained. 'My natural movement is back and across; I don't need to go too deep. On these wickets, you need your back foot play. It has to be my best ODI hundred. Not just the way I batted, given the situation we were in, the desperation with which we needed the bonus point, and the kind of score we were chasing in forty overs.' The bonus point was gained in style as India won to stay afloat but failed to make it to the final since Sri Lanka beat Australia in its next match.

Virat's exceptional form that evening at Hobart brought back memories of West Indian great Viv Richards, who would decimate the bowlers with minimal footwork. Richards could spot the ball early and swing into position to reap the best result. He was a stunning figure at the crease, with a nonchalant expression on his face and his bat spitting fire. No wonder Richards was so generous when talking about Virat. 'I love watching Virat Kohli bat. He looks to me like an individual after my own heart. I love his aggression, and (he has) serious passion that I used to have. He reminds me of myself,' Richards told PTI. 'He is an individual who doesn't back off from confrontation, someone who can stand his ground under pressure. I love that as you can't teach these instinctive aspects of the game. Obviously, once Sachin (Tendulkar) retires, you can bank on Kohli as he is young enough and has a lot of time on his side. He will only improve and continue to get better,' added Richards. Suffice it to say, he was spot on.

Virat was fast-tracked into the Indian one-day squad, on the basis of his batting on a tour to Australia for the Emerging Players Tournament. A place in the team for the Sri Lankan tour gave him five matches. A score of 54 in the fourth match at the R. Premadasa Stadium was a big morale booster for him. He now began to feel that he belonged to the stage. His progress was steady and an unbeaten 79 against the West Indies, at Johannesburg in the 2009 Champions Trophy, was quite a rewarding experience. It also brought him his first Man of the Match honour and Virat justifiably celebrated his arrival in the big league.

His maiden century was not far away, and came at the majestic Eden Gardens, during a series against Sri Lanka. India faced an imposing target of 316 and accomplished it through Gambhir's sensational knock of 150 not out. India sealed the series with a 3-1 margin, with Virat and Gambhir posting 224 for the third wicket. This was after losing Tendulkar and skipper Sehwag for 23 by the fourth over. Virat's 107 was an enjoyable exhibition of stroke play, even though Gambhir ran away with the accolades. Sehwag praised Virat profusely, 'Kohli has done well. He got fifties in the Champions Trophy and against Sri Lanka in his last game. We all knew he had the talent and it was just a matter of performing at the international level.'

For Dinesh Karthik, the wicketkeeper batsman, who spent a lot of time with Virat in the middle, the early success that he gained was not a surprise. 'He had come to the team with a reputation of being a stroke-player on all kind of pitches. People were talking about him and I saw him play some shots with great punch during that century. The way he picked the balls to hit, showed he was quite mature and that raised the bar on and off the field. The discipline levels decide your cricket these days and he was ahead of the rest. His fitness on the field and the lifestyle off it has started a trend for sure. He has set high standards of competition for others to follow and his rise has solid roots in that century at the Eden Gardens,' said Karthik, who had watched Virat's innings from the dressing room.

When India travelled to Bangladesh for a tri-nation tournament in January 2010, Virat grabbed the opportunity to score an unbeaten 102 against the home team. At the post-match press conference, he offered an insight into his maturity as a player. Referring to criticism regarding his attitude during the IPL, he admitted, 'What people said about my attitude during the first IPL was right to a certain extent. I have accepted the criticism and tried to take it in the right spirit. There are two ways to deal with it; you either ignore it or keep continuing in the same way, doing the same mistakes, or you can accept the criticism and rectify it. And I took the second approach.' Few young men would have accepted criticism in such a healthy manner because Virat continues to be a keen learner.

Virat gave his family, coach, and seniors like Dravid and Anil Kumble, the credit for the new phase in his career, a phase which brought a spirit of competitiveness to his game. 'They sensed that something might be going wrong with me and stood by me and supported me. They made me understand the sacrifices that you have to make to do well in international cricket. I have been lucky that way with the people; they have all tried to help me become better,' observed Virat.

He recalled his development, as a responsible batsman, following the experience gained in the Emerging Players Tournament. 'That boosted my confidence tremendously. I just became mentally stronger. I have now learned to bat in high pressure conditions. From that time, I have just been concentrating on my game and not thinking about other things. I am focused now,' said Virat. He has kept true to his words and maintained the focus that helped cement his position in the squad.

The World Cup gave Virat's confidence a huge boost. He was to become a part of history, as India won the Cup for the second time. Gambhir and Dhoni gave the finishing touches to a job that was well begun by Virat, with a knock of 100 not out against Bangladesh, in the opening game of the tournament at Dhaka. Virat could not have asked for a better World Cup debut as he watched Sehwag's fireworks on the other end. Sehwag hit 175 and buried Bangladesh under an avalanche of astounding shots. Talking about the 203-run third wicket association with Virat, he said, 'He is a quick learner, and a mature batsman.' Those words from Sehwag made a world of difference to Virat's approach and he has ensured that bowlers come to earn his wicket.

With the tag of world champion, India travelled to England where Virat crafted a brilliant 107 at Cardiff. His first century against England coincided with Dravid's farewell from ODI cricket after 344 matches and 10889 runs along with 12 centuries. The mantle was being passed on in a significant manner, with the young brigade ready to take over from the seniors. Especially, Virat, the most consistent among the newcomers.

Two years after that hundred at Cardiff, Virat produced a gem at Jaipur that stood out for its ferocity when the team needed it most. An unbeaten 100 against Australia, in the company of a marauding Rohit and Dhawan, showed he had made big strides and deserved to be counted among a galaxy of stars like Dhoni, Yuvraj and Raina, for his individual brilliance. Nine centuries between Cardiff and Jaipur had established Virat's position in the team and nothing could now stop him from claiming his rightful place among the world's elite.

Virat's sixteenth century, as India chased 360 on a wonderful night at Jaipur, was simply breathtaking even as Dhawan (95) and Rohit

(141 not out) made a mockery of the Aussie attack of Mitchell Johnson, Clint McKay, Shane Watson and James Faulkner. The target was same as in the 2003 World Cup final at Johannesburg, but Indian cricket had enormously improved since then. Virat's century off 52 deliveries was the quickest by an India batsman – beating Sehwag's hundred off 60 balls against New Zealand in Hamilton. The Australian skipper aptly put it when he said, 'Virat started attacking us from ball one, but never took any risks which would have helped us come back into the game. He set the tempo and that was smart cricket from him. Basically, all three of them (Virat, Dhawan and Rohit) batted amazingly, but it was Virat who took the game away from us.'

As Dhoni finishes the final lap of his career, the rest of the young team will look to Virat, with India's hopes resting on his leadership qualities. Critics are convinced that Virat should lead the team in all formats of the game, but Virat is not in a hurry. Time is on his side and knowing Virat, he will leave no stone unturned to prepare for the role.

12

A Committed Cricketer

The 2009-10 season produced some fiercely contested games and Delhi did well to reach the semi-finals. However, it lost to a far-superior Mumbai at the Wankhede Stadium. Mumbai went on to win the title with a pulsating six-run win over Karnataka in the final at Mysore.

Delhi had not fielded such a weak team in many years and skipper Rajat Bhatia had a task at hand. Especially, considering that Virat was not available due to India's participation in a tri-series in Bangladesh. No one was surprised at Delhi's loss to Mumbai, but Bhatia was deeply disappointed. Virat, appointed the Delhi captain in recognition of his status at the senior level, had shown exemplary leadership qualities and was convinced that the team possessed the necessary ammunition for the battle ahead. He had demonstrated his fierce desire during the league contest against Maharashtra.

It was a Ranji Trophy match of great consequence for Delhi. The host had ordered a green pitch at the Roshanara Club ground, with an eye on collecting full points against Maharashtra. Virat demonstrated his resilience by leading with the belligerence that marked his cricket, as he fielded and batted. He was charged up throughout the match and nothing highlighted his commitment more than the decision to open the innings in order to help Delhi gain a bonus point.

After the Ferozeshah Kotla, where he had made eight first-class appearances, Virat played five matches at the Roshanara Club, in north Delhi, a venue characterised by an old-world charm. Delhi secured a first-innings lead of 256 runs, but Maharashtra put up a better display in the second innings to avoid an innings defeat. The target was 108 and Virat was confident that a bonus point was possible. Delhi had to make the runs without losing a wicket. It accomplished the feat through Virat and Manhas, with the latter being asked to open the innings in a rare role.

'I just watched him take charge like a true captain. He had read the situation and knew his responsibility. It was important not to lose a wicket, but Virat simply tore into the bowling. He was keen to finish the match and appeared in a hurry to do so,' recalled Manhas, who made a 38 in comparison to Virat's 67 with eleven fours. 'This level of commitment to the team set Virat apart from the rest. He was at ease against pace and spin and all his hard work of junior cricket was paying rich dividends,' added Manhas.

Virat's hunger for runs matched his aggressive instincts. His adaptability left the seniors in awe of the young Virat. He would quickly grasp the instructions with a smile and be ready for the challenge. 'He is a very good student of the game. A silent observer, he always wanted to perform. It's true that everyone wants to perform, but Virat was driven to win at any cost. He was good with his basics and it always helped the team,' said Manhas.

His presence in the dressing room brought about a refreshing change in the Delhi approach to cricket.

'Virat made his debut when I was still playing for Delhi and I have some wonderful memories of him since the day we first met. Virat was always a happy young man full of energy and always keen to be part of a winning side, the dressing room would light up as he always made everyone know he was around. He was a fighter from the beginning and it did not matter if it was a warm-up game of football or volleyball. He always wanted to win. Another great quality of Virat was the respect he had for his seniors in the dressing room and how much he wanted to learn about the game and life from each individual. He always had something to ask of everyone. I have not come across a player as intense as Virat,' said Kuunal Lall, a former Delhi left-arm seamer.

The Delhi team realised that Virat always lived in the present. He never took things lightly, and took care not to lose his temper if he found anyone lacking in effort on the field. 'A very practical man,' was Manhas' remark. Over the years Virat may have mellowed, but his audacity to experiment and raise his game has always been a strong part of his cricket grooming. He always looks towards giving more of himself to his game and does not refrain from punishing his body in trying to achieve that. Although his sense of humour is such that he ably mimics some of his seniors' mannerisms, he also knows how to pick up their cricketing acumen, and emerges as a strong individual, both on and off the field.

On the domestic circuit, Virat brought a strong competitive zeal to his cricket. He would never be satisfied. Even after a victory, he sought the help of his coaches to work on a few shortcomings with intense sessions in the nets. 'I have not seen him resting on his laurels. His overconfidence was transformed into priceless maturity as he progressed and his development was complete through the realisation that he was made to play long in the highest grade of cricket. He had set his goals and nothing was going to stop him from achieving them,' said Bhatia.

That Virat wanted to be the Man of the Moment was well known in the Delhi dressing room. He was a star in every sense. He was playing for India, but hardly imposed his heightened status on his colleagues, some of them in their first season. Virat had learnt the hard way and he was not going to hurt any youngster with a public rebuke. If he had an issue, it would be discussed in private.

Ace India fast bowler Nehra watched Virat grow in the domestic circuit with rare application to the role assigned to him. 'I did not see him waste his time. If not on the field, he would be busy in the gym. I saw him first as a chubby-cheeked bubbly young kid who grew into a perfect athlete. His junior cricket lessons have obviously helped him. I did not know him well, but had heard a lot about his exploits in junior cricket,' recounted Nehra.

Nehra insisted that Virat had changed after the 2011 World Cup. 'The time he spent with the seniors made him realise he was destined to play a bigger role in Indian cricket. I could see his desire to perform in every game. People talked about Rohit's amazing talent to score with lazy grace, but Virat was all the time preparing himself for bigger deeds. Virat was the most professional individual in the Indian dressing room and did well to work on his fitness and game. His disciplined food habits have contributed hugely to keep him battle-ready. Light on his feet meant Virat could respond to a situation with alacrity,' observed Nehra.

His cricket remained on the rise after 2011. It rose even as Virat came to cement his place at No. 3. He was lucky to get the No. 3 and No. 4 spots at a time when he was in tremendous form. He grabbed the chance because it kept the focus on him and also allowed him the space to gauge the situation before launching his assault. Virat knew the recipe to scoring runs in the fifty-over format, and he built on his good form to earn the admiration of the selectors and the team management.

Nehra gave an example to underscore Virat's desire to improve. It was actually his commitment to the game that provided the impetus to excel for Virat. 'After the 2003 World Cup, when I did well, I took things for granted. I thought I was the king of the ring. I ought to have worked hard. Virat did that and took his cricket to a different level after the 2011 World Cup,' Nehra had remarked.

The World Cup over, Virat concentrated on his fitness and that made him a special player. His batting evolved and he learnt to value his success. He excelled on the field and celebrated it in the gym. His success has not slowed his progress and it has rubbed off on his colleagues in the team. The significance of grooming was underlined by the difference between Tendulkar and Vinod Kambli. The latter was as big a star as Tendulkar, but failed in the absence of proper grooming. Success did not rest well on Kambli's shoulders and the lack of application was evident in his cricket which grew rapidly and then collapsed beyond repair.

At the end of every series, at home or abroad, at the end of a difficult match, Virat made it a point to introspect. At the end of a happy outing too he analysed his game to clearly identify the plus and minus points. His coach was his guide. 'We would discuss the issues over the phone for hours and in the nets at the Academy whenever possible. I saw the same commitment that I had seen earlier when he was ten years of age. His aggression had been tempered over a period of time, but not his passion to be in the centre of action,' said Raj Kumar.

There was a time when Raj Kumar was worried about his pupil going astray. The under-19 World Cup triumph at Kuala Lumpur had brought Virat unprecedented fame and there was a distinct change in his behaviour. He was seen as brash, but not at the cost of his discipline. Virat had never been accused of indiscipline in his junior days and once he wore the India colours, he learnt to maintain his cool in explosive situations. As an eighteen-year-old, Virat was not different from any other boy next door who wanted to have fun. Fame had transformed his life. He was picked up by RCB for IPL and distractions came to threaten his game and slow down his development. There was a lot of partying and since he was a star, Virat's presence at such events became part of the RCB cricket culture, which was a sharp contrast to the Mumbai Indian's uncompromising policy to sponsor its team's post-match celebrations. The BCCI subsequently put a stop to these private parties organised by the franchises.

There is an interesting anecdote involving Virat and the franchise when he demanded a

Business Class ticket for himself because a senior India player had availed of that facility. It did not matter if Virat was refused the luxury of travelling Business Class, but it became clear that the young man was going to demand what was due to him. It was true that Virat would not take nonsense from anyone because he was aware of his position and rights.

Virat's coach played his part superbly. 'My role required strict supervision because I had seen many youngsters spoilt by early fame. I was never really worried about Virat, but I had to be careful. He was young and I decided to spend more and more time with him. Kept an eye on him,' said the coach.

A senior Delhi and India player was instrumental in making Raj Kumar realise the importance of shepherding his talented and star student. 'Reign him in,' the player told Raj Kumar. Virat quickly recovered to regain his focus. He knew the star that he had become was because of cricket. Nothing else mattered and the lesson was learnt in quick time. 'He was never insolent. He was aggressive, but never disrespectful,' affirmed Nehra.

Confidence was erroneously portrayed as arrogance in Virat's case. The confidence to pull off a miraculous result was his strength. Virat made no attempt to hide his passion. A bouncer would evoke a strong response like stepping out the next ball. 'I would shout to him to stay calm if someone bounced the ball because I was sure Virat would step out next ball to hit the bowler. It was aggression and not arrogance. It was confidence,' insisted Raj Kumar.

As Virat rose in stature, Raj Kumar tightened his observation. 'I reminded him once in a while that everything would follow provided he never compromised with his cricket. The hard work of the Academy would go to dust if he made mistakes after having established himself. It was stressful only for a brief while because I always knew Virat was not the one to go astray,' Raj Kumar said with pride.

For his elevation to captaincy at Delhi, Virat had former Bihar and Delhi batsman Hari Gidwani to thank. Gidwani was a stylish right-hander who was unfortunate not to have played for India. Gidwani was a conscientious selector and chiefly instrumental in pushing Virat as the best candidate to lead Delhi. Gidwani convinced his colleagues in the panel to appoint the twenty-one-year-old Virat. 'I backed him because I had heard about him and then seen him lead in the Under-19 World Cup at Kuala Lumpur. He came across as a brilliant communicator and that was the quality a captain needed the most,' said Gidwani.

Virat transformed the atmosphere in the dressing room. There was freedom for all to express their opinion. He had never believed in imposing his views and came off as a friendly yet firm leader. 'I saw him grow within a short span of time. His batting was breathtaking, even though he was yet to play a Test match. I am old-fashioned and strongly believe that only Test cricket brings out the best in a player. He has to be a technically good batsman to excel in Test cricket,' Gidwani said.

Virat batted like a champion for Delhi. With a straight bat, he would drive the ball to mid-wicket and mid-on. It was a spectacle worth watching. His back foot play was tremendous. The punch would send the ball whistling to the boundary. It became his trademark stroke. His cricket was an eye-opener and a great learning process for his teammates. 'My only concern about Virat was his anger and hyperactivity. But what a remarkable transformation he has brought to himself and the Indian team,' noted Gidwani.

Taken together, Virat has played twenty-three Ranji Trophy matches for Delhi. The last one resulted in a crushing defeat at the Nehru Stadium in Ghaziabad in 2012, when Uttar Pradesh won by six wickets. Delhi's star-studded batting line-up comprising Sehwag, Gambhir, Virat, Unmukt and Manhas succumbed on a seaming pitch. Sehwag's century in the second innings was the lone redeeming feature for Delhi. Virat's contribution was 14 and 43, consumed by seamer Bhuvneshwar, on both the occasions.

International engagements kept Virat busy and he was lost to Delhi cricket. Some of the local tournament organisers fondly remember

Virat gracing their venues during his formative years. Pramod Sood reflected, 'Virat played in our tournament at the Guru Gobind Singh College ground (in April 2005). He made a scintillating 113 not out for Vidya Jain Club against Malviya Club. Sadly, he ended up in the losing camp despite an outstanding innings. It is nice to see him grow in international cricket. What I remember from that match was his commitment. He came across as a well-behaved kid,' said Sood. Eleven years down the line, Virat has not changed. His dedication to cricket has not diminished. He also remains a simple man at heart for the cricketing fraternity, his love for the game a byword for his commitment.

13

Leadership

He is the guiding spirit of Indian cricket, in the post-Tendulkar period. Heroes and icons, emerging in different eras, have enriched the history of cricket, giving the game a fillip to compete with other sports. Virat is the uncrowned king of modern cricket, as he scales new peaks in every season and in all formats of the game. Is he the complete batsman for whom we have waited all this time? The answer will reveal itself in due course, as Virat leads India with rare distinction – a century in his first Test as captain against Australia, Sri Lanka and the West Indies.

Cricket has been deemed a gentleman's game. It was certainly one from the times of Charles Bannerman and Victor Trumper, to Donald Bradman, Denis Compton, Frank Worrell and Garry Sobers. However, it failed to acquire a global image and remained confined to nations with a colonial past. In this regard, a cricketer like Virat has the potential to not only sustain the interest of the masses in the longer form of cricket – Tests – but also become the brand ambassador in popularizing the other formats of the game across the world.

Cricketers from different times have hailed Virat as the player of the generation. For the best of prose writers to shower encomiums on Virat would be a tempting exercise because he sets new benchmarks and challenges himself to improve every time he walks to the middle. Cricket has seen some legendary leaders who took the responsibility to deliver, when faced with the most formidable situations, early or late in their career.

Worrell and Richie Benaud come to mind instantly for bringing dignity to the job of captaincy. The 1960-61 series between Australia and the West Indies was a hallmark phase in international cricket. The two teams produced epic contests – including the tied Test at Brisbane, the first in 498 matches. Virat has assumed the reigns of captaincy in times when teams look to stifle the opposition through all possible means, within the laws of the game, as Test cricket faces the test for its own survival.

Leaders are born, not made, goes the saying. Take Imran Khan for instance. He transformed the face of Pakistan cricket with his leadership. His word was law in the dressing room, and he was able to extract the best out of his team by walking the talk. He took the first step and they followed with inspiring acts. Pakistan cricket was at its peak when Imran was at the helm.

The 1992 World Cup triumph in Australia was a golden moment in Pakistan's cricket history, and the credit largely, and justifiably, went to Imran. He was able to convince his players that they had the potential to become world champions. Virat has a similar streak, the ability to motivate his team through his game and stimulating captaincy.

Virat's transition to the top job in Indian cricket has not been an overnight exercise. He was always the captain in waiting. Whether playing club cricket or engaged on the domestic circuit, he was the most intense character on the field, at times hyperactive, but always committed to giving his best and spurring his teammates to give their best.

As a captain, Mike Brearley of England left a mark on cricket, with his ability to control the pace and preserve the spirit of the game. He is credited with being the motivator for Ian Botham, helping him to come up with some stunning all-round feats. The English rated him as one of the finest captains, a born leader, who knew his job like a veteran surgeon in the operation theatre. Virat is still learning the basics of captaincy, but appears set to lead the team into a zone where invincibility could well become a reality.

His elevation as captain hardly surprised those who had followed Virat's career from his youngster days. 'One got very positive vibes from him. I can't remember Virat ever shouting at the bowlers if they erred. He always backed his players, always, and that helped in ensuring the team gave its best,' recalled Delhi all-rounder Sumit Narwal, also Virat's colleague at the Oil and Natural Gas Corporation (ONGC).

Much before he led India, Virat had shown promise at the domestic level. 'I remember we had given away too many runs against Saurashtra (in Ranji Trophy), at the Roshanara Club ground (in 2009). He spoke to every bowler and talked about a recovery in the second innings. We went on to win the match. Delhi had some new faces in the squad, but Virat treated them with respect. His remarkable captaincy is what I remember the most from that match,' said Narwal.

Virat is a captain who involves himself in every activity when on the field. From shining the ball, or rushing to hand over the bowler's cap to the umpire, he appears to be the busiest man. There is a tendency in him to be in the thick of action. If there is pressure building up, Virat emerges as the man to deal with the situation. As a captain, he takes every responsibility on his shoulders.

A sure sign of a good captain is his desire to learn. Virat is a quick learner, and learns quicker when it comes to implementing the knowledge that he has acquired through a practical process. He does not fear experimenting even in tight situations because that, he firmly believes, is the way forward. In an interview with *The Hindu,* he gave a glimpse of his leadership qualities in a brief analysis that reflected his approach to the job.

'As a captain, I always tell my teammates that I will never ask them to do something that I can't do first. For example, during that Test in Adelaide, the night before the fifth day, I gathered everyone and told them we were going for the target. If I say that and the next day I go out and make 20 runs in 80 balls...that does not connect me to the team. I first convince myself if I can do it, and only then I ask my teammates to go for it. When everyone is working hard and someone takes things for granted, I do speak to him. He is bound to realise his mistake when there is an atmosphere of honesty in the dressing room,' Virat explained his stand. Australia won that Test, as India, set a target of 364 runs, fell short by 48 runs despite Virat's brilliant knock of 141, his second century of the Test match.

Pataudi is counted among the best captains India has seen. He taught the team how to play to win. 'Draw can be a good result, but a victory is to be cherished,' Pataudi had once said. He was only twenty-one when he was handed the job, on a tour to the West Indies in 1962, ahead of stalwarts in the team like Polly Umrigar, Chandu Borde and Vijay Manjrekar. The captain on that tour, Nari Contractor, was felled by a terrible bouncer from Charlie Griffith and Pataudi found himself saddled with the most difficult job in Indian cricket. Pataudi wrote later that cricket was a hard game to be played hard by men by using a hard ball. But it is only a game, he had reminded us, before passing over the role to Ajit Wadekar.

Captaincy comes with immense responsibility. Pataudi accepted the job, even as the team was going through a transition. Just as Virat, who started by sharing the dressing room with performers like Tendulkar, Dravid, Laxman, Sehwag and Kumble. When appointed the captain, after Dhoni relinquished the mantle in a huff, Virat found himself leading a young bunch that looked up to him for guidance. Pataudi always insisted that a captain had to command the players' respect, and to do that he had to perform. Virat's approach to the job is inspired by Pataudi's mantra, who did not believe in being aloof and preferred to be known as a sociable captain.

Virat is playing in times when intense media scrutiny adds to the pressure of an international cricketer. A sharp contrast to when Bedi, Gavaskar and Kapil, addressed a media gathering of not more than ten. They dealt with the opposition differently, but the focus was always on keeping the record clean. They had their strengths and weaknesses, along with an uncompromising attitude when it came to standing up for players' interests. Bedi was the most vocal as a captain, while Gavaskar and Kapil too did not refrain from airing their complaints. In Virat's case, the circumstances have undergone a massive change. There is little to protest against, as he has the backing of the Board and the National selectors.

A captain has to be attuned to each and every aspect of the game and his team. When Virat is around, the players can rest assured that they have the freedom to pick his brains on all aspects of the game. He loves to discuss, a confirmation of a captain's desire to understand his team. Opponents are known to praise Virat, who has come to temper his anger on the field. Captaincy has mellowed Virat, but not to the extent where the opponents, or for that matter his mates, can take him for granted.

Gavaskar was known for his meticulous homework preceding a match. Those were the days devoid of technical support from a staff that today comprises a coach and his assistants, including a trainer, physiotherapist and video analyst. Gavaskar also did not leave the job to others. A fine reading of the game was Gavaskar's forte. He was sometimes compelled to adopt defensive measures, but not Bedi, who did not mind living by the sword. 'I realised early that winning was important for a captain. Only if we did not stand a chance to win did I approve of playing for a draw,' Bedi stressed on his way of leading the team.

Virat follows in the tradition of Kapil's methods. Both share the trait to lead by instinct, and prioritise their own good performance to set an example. 'I like Virat's style,' said Kapil. 'He makes no effort to hide his aggression and that conveys the team's attitude too. He wants to win. Unless a captain shows a positive approach, the team faces the possibility of playing below potential. He understands the importance and responsibility of a captain very well, probably the best in a long time. Let us not compare him to Dhoni, who I considered to be unique. Dhoni made mistakes and learnt.' However, when insisted upon to compare Dhoni with Virat at an event, Kapil had jokingly remarked, 'Father can't be compared to his son. Can he? Father will always remain father.'

During Gavaskar and Bedi's active playing days, an individual's capacity to lead the team was measured purely by his performance in domestic cricket, which was confined to the Ranji Trophy and Duleep Trophy. Virat first showed his talent at captaincy in junior cricket and led Delhi in mere two first-class matches. 'We had our limitations. We also made mistakes. But we made every effort to learn from our seniors. I made lot of mistakes and I have no qualms in admitting that. I can see that Virat has grown as a leader. He leaves nothing to chance and that is the best way to lead the team, by grabbing the opportunity. Of course he has a long way to go as a captain. I hope Virat stays grounded and looks to learn every time he leads the team on to the field. He looks promising enough to be India's finest captain no doubt,' said Kapil.

There was a distinct change in the team's attitude from the time Dhoni took over. His calm demeanour even under pressure was a standout quality. Virat is different. He loves to demonstrate his passion, while taking charge of the situation. Dhoni was adept at hiding his disappointment. No such thing for Virat, who makes no secret of his likes and dislikes. 'Nothing wrong with that. Every captain has his favourites,' insists Bedi. 'But he must take care not to harbour ill feelings within the team.'

Virat has the honesty to be hailed as a leader. A leader has to think for the team, and Virat is never one to shy away from such a daunting task. He is the mostly likely member in the squad to lose his sleep for the sake of his colleagues. 'Look at how he runs his partner's singles. As if his life depends on it. He is constantly worrying about his teammates. He is a caring captain,' said Nehra, who knew Virat even before he had made his under-15 debut for Delhi.

A player's captain. That is how Virat would like to be known. He had admitted that man management was not an easy 'skill,' but he seems to be on the right track. 'You have to start with a blank mind, understand the individual and set aside your ego,' was his candid view of things. India can look forward to an unprecedented era of dominance in world cricket, under the astute leadership of this player's captain.

14

The World at His Feet

There was a lot of anticipation in the air, and it was not unfounded. The elite of world cricket was arriving in India to showcase its potential in the shortest format of the game. T20 may have irked the purists, but the young generation seemed to have embraced the entertainment aspect of cricket. The IPL has obviously influenced this particular format of the game, and raised the expectations from the home team, which meant the tournament was lapped up by all and sundry.

The home team was the favourite for many reasons, and Virat was a prime one, given his capacity to carry the game beyond the ordinary. In a team game, an individual cannot always make a difference, but Virat is full of surprises. He was the darling of the nation, and a firm believer in his talent and capacity to deliver. He had made massive strides in the season preceding the ICC World Twenty20 and the stage was set for him – home conditions and his present form making for a lethal combination.

C.K. Nayudu, Vijay Merchant, Pataudi, G.R. Viswanath, Gavaskar, Tendulkar, Bedi, Kapil, Sehwag, Kumble, Laxman, Dravid and Dhoni were among the prominent ones who have shaped Indian cricket's destiny over the years. The arrival of Virat signalled a change in the attitude and approach of the team. There was a palpable form of forcefulness in all formats of the game and a distinct aura of self-belief in the team. The team, led by the enviably talented Virat, inculcated a drive to win, going on the offensive. The ICC World Twenty20 was seen as a stage that India was expected to dominate and ultimately conquer. It was because of a certain Virat Kohli, charging ahead in an imperious manner.

There was drama in the run-up to the tournament when Pakistan held back its team, demanding security assurances from the Indian government. The International Cricket Council (ICC) had taken care not to schedule Pakistan's matches in Mumbai, as the organisers anticipated trouble and protests during games featuring the team. Given the status of the competition, Pakistan could not have dared to skip the tournament, considering it was an ICC event with India providing the facilities to stage it. Pakistan, sensibly and also under pressure from the world of cricket, eventually relented and the tournament took off. Indian fans firmly supported their team to win the title it had won in 2007.

Virat and Joe Root, two batsmen who prove to be your money's worth, were expected to spearhead their respective team's batting strength. The bowlers obviously dreaded running into them when on song. The common thread was their technical brilliance and the ability to adapt to all the three formats. At the end of the ICC World Twenty20, Virat and Root emerged with their reputations enhanced though the crown went to the West Indies. The West Indies team was the most under-rated combination, in spite of the fact that it had some of the most explosive batsmen at its command.

In a competition where robust hitting was the accepted practice, Virat and Root demonstrated the benefits of playing by the book. Virat was in exceptional form, and he continued to grow in stature as the tournament progressed. He loves to make a statement and works to create a foundation for the same. From the first ball he faced, Virat made his intentions known. He was going to be a busy man at the crease.

There was much hype around batsmen like Gayle, de Villiers and Glenn Maxwell. They had the well-tested capacity to swing the game on their own, but all of them lacked the consistency to be counted among the big-match finishers. The innovative character of their batting style led critics to believe that Gayle, de Villiers and Maxwell would be the batsmen to excel. As things transpired, it was Virat who stole the limelight, with his batting that drew its strength from sound temperament.

India was rated high on the strength of its batting depth. With Dhoni around and batsmen like Virat, Dhawan, Rohit, Yuvraj and Raina, the team boasted of a powerful run-making line-up. Virat, of course, was the leader of the pack with his forte being the astonishing trait of playing the big innings. Virat can not only face up to the best in the game, but also produce his best to make a strong point. There is no word such as 'defeat' in his dictionary.

However, it was a disappointing start for Virat, when he was foxed by leg-spinner Ish Sodhi, at the opener at Nagpur against New Zealand. The pitch assisted the spinners and India suffered an ignominious loss when it failed to chase down 127. Mitchell Santner, a 24-year-old left-arm spinner from Hamilton and the 23-year-old Sodhi, a Ludhiana-born first generation immigrant settled in Auckland, left India in an embarrassing state.

Virat was stung by the dismissal and the defeat. He was adept at playing spin, but in this case, he had failed his team. He had fallen to Sodhi's first ball, which was unlike his natural game of closely studying the bowler before launching a tirade against him. Sodhi spun the ball furiously and Virat's ambitious cover-drive merely picked an edge. It was a poor start by any standard.

India and Virat made amends in the next outing – the marquee match against Pakistan. The venue of the match had been shifted from Dharamsala to Kolkata due to the local government's inability to give an assurance of security to the visiting team. It was a black spot on the cricket administrators and led to a huge dent in revenue for local businesses in the hilly town. The hotels suffered losses from late cancellations and the cricket fans felt let down. The last-minute change in the venue caused hardships to those connected with the organisation of the match at this most scenic of cricket grounds.

India had a record to maintain – of never having lost to Pakistan in a World Cup meeting in both formats (fifty overs and Twenty20) – and there was no change in the script as Virat produced an attractive 55 and Pakistan was thrashed by six wickets. It was a difficult feat to achieve. India, in pursuit of 119 to win the rain-affected match, was reduced to 23 for 3 when Virat was joined in the middle order by Yuvraj, a match-winner in his own right.

There were early indications of Virat's form and Eden Gardens was witness to some of his sublime artistry during that match-deciding knock. Especially, in executing the cover-drives, most tactically placed, and playing the ball late, Virat showed how quickly he adapted to the task. Virat really loves it when he is confronted with tough conditions, and the pitch at Eden Gardens tested a batsman's technique and range of strokes. Virat produced them in plenty and was able to quell Pakistan's ambitions of an upset win.

Upon the completion of his half-century, Virat bowed to a certain cricket icon he had admired all his life – Tendulkar. It was an impromptu act that reflected his love for Tendulkar and his own humility. He wanted to share the glory with the man who had inspired him to play cricket. The world watched as Virat's obeisance to Tendulkar, sitting in the galleries, offered a glimpse of his humble persona. This was an act of reverence that touched Tendulkar's heart, and he responded with a warm smile for his most committed fan.

The Eden Gardens had witnessed some of the most magnificent batting shows in the past, notably from wrist masters like Viswanath, Mohammad Azharuddin and Laxman. Virat's display was equally worthy of finding a place among the best at this grand venue. Although of a short duration, it had a lasting impact.

There was another individual for the discerning cricket enthusiast's eye – Pakistan's Mohammed Amir, who was returning to competitive cricket after serving a five-year ban for spot fixing. He made an instant impact on the cricket world with a lively spell against Bangladesh – picking his first wicket with a fiery delivery and the next with a slower one.

Amir was sensational against India too, conceding just eleven runs in three overs, teasing and tormenting the batsmen with his guile. He may not have helped Pakistan go past the league stage, but did enough to merit a gift from the reigning champion of the cricket world. The bat that Virat presented Amir must indeed be a treasure for the young Pakistani fast bowler. This gesture was symbolic of the fact that the cricketing fraternity had welcomed Amir back into the fold and was willing to let bygones be bygones.

Having snatched the game away from Pakistan, Virat was ready to fire again when India met Bangladesh in Bangalore. The home team escaped by a one-run margin, thanks to the Bangladesh batsmen, who failed to feast on the juicy full tosses by Hardik Pandya in the last over of the game. It was a bad last-over choice by Dhoni and Pandya ended up being a hero simply because Mahmudullah and Mushfiqur Rahim could not get two runs off three poor balls.

India had struggled to compile 146 off twenty overs and Virat had contributed a paltry 24 before getting out on a clumsy sweep. The win meant India had managed to stay in the hunt and there was still scope for Virat to build on his splendid start against Bangladesh. The breath-taking knock against Australia was proof of Virat's fierce desire to win and demonstrate his passion for the game.

There was nothing unconventional about his batting against Australia. In spite of being the shortest format, his innings was so deftly constructed that it seemed to have shades of a Test match special. This was Virat at his magical best. Call it sublime, artistic, or methodical demolition of the opposition, it deserved a place among the best. It was an innings that any batsman would have been proud to emulate.

This was easily *the* innings of the tournament. It is true that Carlos Braithwaite left an indelible impression with his four sixes in a row to finish the final and give West Indies a memorable win over England. But Virat's performance in Mohali was quite extraordinary. It earned itself a slot in cricket folklore.

Batting maestro Gavaskar was in a state of rapture on air. He was like a fan watching as his hero exploded on the big stage, pulling off one entertaining stroke after another. 'Fantabulous', Gavaskar exclaimed at a cover-drive, which Virat produced with a literally straight bat, tilting it just a trifle and giving the ball the direction he desired. Virat's elbow and head position was just what the coaching manual would have recommended.

'It was tremendous batting effort from him, superb batting. Especially the areas where you want to score runs, where you want to play big shots. I think more often than not, it is about selection of shots and execution of shots. I feel overall, Virat was very good not just with his stroke play but also in the running between the wickets – you take minimum risk if you can run fast,' said Dhoni on Virat's show.

For Dhoni to concede Virat's stupendous feat as a runner was a remarkable achievement in itself. It came from a man who has been acknowledged by experts of the game as one of the finest judges of a run in modern cricket. Virat was not only the toast of the team, but also the nation, and rightly so. This was a showpiece knock in a campaign where India had managed to keep afloat, winning by a whisker against Bangladesh, and successfully taming Australia in a knock-out contest.

'It certainly has to be in the top three,' Kohli said of his innings at the post-match presentation. 'Probably the top right now because I'm a bit emotional. I would like to put this on top. Against Australia, a world-class side, literally a quarter-final for us, we had to go over the line. There's a lot riding on us in this World Cup, we are playing at home and the crowds want to see us, and we just want to give them as much entertainment and fun as possible.'

These thoughts conveyed how much Virat valued the innings. 'I don't really know what to say right now because I'm overwhelmed by the position we were in and then to take out the match. This is what you play cricket for. You need new challenges in every game. Trust me, you don't like these situations too much.'

Cricket, like any other sport, is also about winning matches. It is not surprising that Virat has played cricket to win matches. That is what the best cricketers do, they combine the will to win matches and enjoy the game while they are at it. Virat was not satisfied with winning the match from a weak position. He transformed the challenge into a show of his physical and mental strength, demonstrating his true potential. He ran as if his life depended on it. Dhoni later joked that Virat ought to 'pay him' for running all the runs. They sprinted with supreme athleticism, recovering their composure and breath in time, and launched into an increasingly aggressive stroke play that left the Australians bewildered.

Virat had trained for this – all the hours spent in the nets, mastering the shots, and the rigorous endurance training – to give him the strength required when running tirelessly. His training held good at this critical stage. His aggregate was 273 runs in five innings, but the manner in which he had belted the attack was remarkable. There was a method to his art of accumulating runs, a restrained aggression – sometimes refraining from the big shots, but biding his time before accelerating.

For this particular innings to have figured among his best meant that it was special. He was the fundamental difference between the teams that night. Australia was off to a stirring start thanks to Usman Khawaja and Aaron Finch. However, a total of 160 proved hard to defend, given Virat's form. Although Australia made early dents by removing Dhawan and Rohit, the presence of Virat ensured the fight was at full throttle.

The semi-final was a fight indeed, and a robust one at that. A replacement player, Lendl Simmons, put India out of the competition with an astonishing charge in the company of Andre Russell, making a mockery of a stiff target of 193. Simmons was flown in to take the place of an injured Andre Fletcher and within two days of landing, he was charting an epic win for his team. From nineteen for two, West Indies cruised to a stunning victory, even as Virat watched with a growing despondency. Virat's unbeaten innings of 89 had been as pristine and artistic as any in the tournament. Yet he ended up in the losing camp because of two bowling follies later in the match.

India let off Simmons twice. First R. Ashwin lured him into presenting a catch at short third man, but to the chagrin of his team, the off-spinner had overstepped. Next, Simmons was out to Pandya, but the bowler had overstepped again and the resultant free-hit was sent sailing over midwicket. The two let offs and the runs hurt in the end when Simmons and Russell demolished the Indian attack with brutal shots. The two slammed ten sixes as India's bowling went to pieces.

For Virat, it was heart-breaking. He had given India a great opportunity with an innings that created the platform for a win. It had proper cricket shots, constructed with care. It had contained some cover-drives that had evoked awe and admiration even from the opposition. Essentially, it was an innings that could have served as a model exhibition of correct batsmanship. Virat had pushed his body to its utmost to run those splendid ones and twos, and created the perfect situation upon which the team should have thrived.

However, India was eliminated on that day by West Indies, a team which was well on its course to winning the title, having derived motivation from being labelled the underdogs of the tournament. The glum countenance of Virat was such a contrast to his vibrant batting. He had done everything that he possibly could have, but the team failed to counter the challenges that arose for the middle order.

Virat is known to absorb pressure, and allow his partner to relax and play his natural game. He is also known to assure his teammates that he would finish the game. He could not wrap up this one because two of the Indian bowlers, in an act described as 'unpardonable' by Kapil, bowled no-balls at critical stages. It is a pity that Virat's individual brilliance did not count in the semi-final whereas West Indies played like a team and finished the job in style.

15

The Icon

Cricket is a simple game, sometimes played by complicated characters. Gentlemen have traditionally held an exalted position in this game, where dissent and bad behaviour are considered to be out of character for a cricketer. The administrators are constantly engaged in exercises to boost the image of cricket and reach out to far corners of the globe. However, cricket is yet to be recognised as a truly global sport. If it has remained confined to countries which had come under colonial influence the reasons can be mainly attributed to its format. The five-day game, especially, has become a cause for concern, contributing towards dwindling attendance and falling standards. It is due to its icons and heroes that cricket has produced over time that the game itself continues to survive.

Bradman was the ultimate cricketer for many. For some, it was Sobers. India rode on the shoulders of Gavaskar and Kapil and both had distinct roles to play. Gavaskar showed the way to

A joyous moment for Shikhar Dhawan and Virat Kohli during the
2015 World Cup match against South Africa at Melbourne.

Photo credit: Suman Chattopadhyay / *Sangbad Pratidin*

Cine actor Akshay Kumar with Virat, the Man of the Match
against Sri Lanka at Dhaka in the 2012 Asia Cup.

Photo credit: Suman Chattopadhyay / *Sangbad Pratidin*

Playing a cover drive in the Test against Australia at Chennai in 2012.
Photo credit: Suman Chattopadhyay / *Sangbad Pratidin*

Batting with Sachin Tendulkar
in the same Test in 2012.
Photo credit:
Suman Chattopadhyay / *Sangbad Pratidin*

Celebrating a dismissal.
Photo credit:
Suman Chattopadhyay / *Sangbad Pratidin*

Team Director Ravi Shastri having a word with Virat.
Photo credit: Suman Chattopadhyay / *Sangbad Pratidin*

With Virender Sehwag after India's victory over Australia in the 2016 T20
World Cup match at Mohali.

Photo credit: Suman Chattopadhyay / *Sangbad Pratidin*

Obliging Bangladeshi fans in Dhaka after the 2011 World Cup match.

Photo credit: Suman Chattopadhyay / *Sangbad Pratidin*

With Pakistan's captain Shahid Afridi at the 2016 T20 World Cup match at the Eden Gardens.

Photo credit: Suman Chattopadhyay / *Sangbad Pratidin*

Consoled by skipper M.S. Dhoni after the T20 World Cup semi-final loss against West Indies at Wankhede Stadium in Mumbai.

Photo credit: Suman Chattopadhyay / *Sangbad Pratidin*

A picture of joy after a satisfactory Test innings.
Photo credit: Suman Chattopadhyay / *Sangbad Pratidin*

Virat with his puppy Bruno at home.
Photo credit: Vijay Lokapally

The Author after an exhaustive interview with Virat at his residence
Photo credit: Vijay Lokapally

bat with courage and dignity, Viswanath and Kapil played the game with unmatched flair. There were heroes like Mohinder Amarnath and Dravid who blunted the opposition with stoic resistance. Artists like Azharuddin and Laxman produced pure entertainment at the crease, and champion bowlers like Kumble and Harbhajan revived the magic of yesteryear idols like Bedi, B.S. Chandrasekhar and E.A.S. Prasanna. One of the biggest stars of the game was Sehwag, whose batting was unparalleled. His irrepressible aggression attracted crowds, filling up the venue, as Sehwag opened the innings in both the longest and shortest formats of the game, and tormented the bowlers around the world. His retirement was much celebrated by the bowlers' fraternity.

The stalwarts departed at various times, leaving a void that was hard to fill. The game itself witnessed an upheaval, with tradition giving way to the demands of present-day spectators who largely preferred the Twenty20 culture to five-day cricket. As a result, the character of the game changed and so did the actors who played varied roles in the three formats – Test, ODI and T20. There was a surge in the number of matches on the domestic and international calendar, with greater emphasis on playing with aggression and producing results. The audience loved result-oriented cricket, which was guaranteed in the limited overs variety. Cricket, as a game, had ceased to be the way that Bradman,

Sobers, Gavaskar and Kapil had pursued. It was far more demanding and far too commercial. Controversies like spot-fixing and match-fixing had tainted cricket. The administrators were concerned at cricket's reputation being damaged and measures were taken to save it from further deterioration.

Cricketers came under intense scrutiny with anti-corruption agencies training their lens on them. The administrators created a wedge between the players and the media. The cricketers felt choked, but they were not the ones to complain. Lucrative contracts and substantial match fees ensured a rosy future for the cricketers, and the introduction of the IPL changed the inherent character of the game. It brought in big money to make the administrators happy. The generation of Tendulkar, Kumble, Dravid and Sehwag did not play for money. The previous lot of Gavaskar, Kapil, Bedi and Prasanna were paid a pittance, compared to the modern stars, who could dream of owning mansions and other luxuries of the rich. Against this background, Indian cricket witnessed the emergence of Virat, a shining pupil of the game, set to rewrite most records and script an exciting way of playing cricket.

A run-accumulator, entertainer, youth icon, entrepreneur, and much more, Virat is a multi-tasking role model. He bats to win. He wins to keep the game going in a nation that is starved of heroes. He is a hero, but cut from a different cloth. He can be brash if the opposition is cheeky. He can also be compassionate, but not when he has a bat in hand. His imperious presence at the crease can leave the opposition demoralised even as his legion of fans grows with every outing. The stadiums would echo 'Sachin, Sachin' not so long back. It is 'Viraaat, Viraaat' that reverberates around the stadiums these days. His brisk gait may suggest that he is a man in a hurry. He is not. Virat plans his cricket meticulously, with short-term goals to be achieved without fail. If in case he fails to achieve them, he sets up a punishing schedule for himself, spending more time in the nets, and with the video analyst, to help him re-construct his game.

Virat is a work in progress. He is an engrossing character, who will fight tooth and nail for his partners, and take on the opposition with a blend of aggression and calmness. Many opponents have discovered his anger—in a verbal dose to assert his presence. He firmly believes in giving it back. His middle-finger wagging act in Australia in 2012 was an example of how Virat would not accept things lying down. Repeatedly taunted by the Sydney crowd, he showed the middle finger. 'I agree cricketers don't have to retaliate. What when the crowd says the worst things about your mother and sister. The worst I've heard, never heard crap like that. EVER,' he had tweeted. He was unrelenting in his stance and this was seen as the new trend in

Indian cricket. There was a place for aggression, and young guns like Virat would not shy away from demonstrating it.

Within a year, Virat once again exploded on the cricket field, but without a bat this time. The Chinnaswamy Stadium witnessed a Virat-Gambhir spat that left the audience stunned. Two Delhi and India teammates going at each other was an unsightly spectacle, but accepted as part of the game in modern times. A cricketer must be seen as an expressive individual on the field, what with the TV cameras following every moment and beaming it across the world. Virat, in this case, was steering RCB to the target of 155 in the IPL clash with Kolkata Knight Riders (KKR), when he lost his wicket.

Having slammed two sixes off Delhi teammate Pradeep Sangwan, also his India under-19 colleague, Virat attempted to slice L. Balaji, but only holed out to Eoin Morgan. As he appeared to walk back to the dressing room, something snapped in him and he moved towards Gambhir, who was equally menacing, while confronting a livid Virat. Things had suddenly taken a turn for the worse. Another Delhi player, Bhatia, fielding at third man, sprinted to the spot of action and separated the two from a potentially explosive situation. 'I felt sad,' was all that Bhatia would say of the incident that portrayed Virat and Gambhir in poor light. Elsewhere, in Delhi, their coaches were also appalled at the development in Bangalore. 'We called each other to ensure that neither of us spoke to the media,' said Gambhir's coach Sanjay Bhardwaj. For Raj Kumar, it was a 'minor' incident and hardly a concern since he knew Gambhir and Virat would soon bury the differences, if there were any. Needless to say there is no love lost between the two.

Virat is not the one to change just for the sake of it. He has always believed in being transparent. He would protest strongly if he saw injustice. During the 2014 England tour, when girlfriend Anushka Sharma stayed in the team hotel, there was a furor in the media. 'Not part of our culture,' screamed the team manager Sunil Dev. However, Virat had taken prior permission, even as needless attention was paid to a private matter. It was not as if Virat had smuggled his girlfriend into the hotel in a clandestine manner. The team was aware and so was the Board of Control for Cricket in India (BCCI). At another point, Virat erred in lashing out at the wrong journalist during the 2015 World Cup in Australia, mistaking him for the one who had written about Anushka's presence in the England team hotel.

The World Cup ended up being a disappointment for Virat when he failed against Australia in the semi-final at Sydney. A bouncer from Johnson climbed on him and his resultant pull was a disaster. His dismissal was uncharitably attributed on social media to the presence of Anushka in the stands.

Soon, she would again be in the news, this time for not attending the Mohali match. The Mohali match was where Virat decimated Australia in the 2016 ICC World Twenty20 with an astonishing innings. Following the trolling of Anushka, it was natural for Virat to respond. He stood by her with a strong and well-articulated message on Twitter and Instagram.

His Instagram post read, 'Shame on those people who have been having a go at Anushka for the longest time and connecting every negative thing to her. Shame on those people calling themselves educated. Shame on blaming and making fun of her when she has no control over what I do with my sport. If anything she has only motivated and given me more positivity. This was long time coming. Shame on these people that hide and take a dig. And I don't need any respect for this post. Have some compassion and respect her. Think of how your sister or girlfriend or wife would feel if someone trolled them and very conveniently rubbished them in public.'

Outside the cricket field, social issues engaged his attention too. In an interview to *The Hindu*, he spoke about gender equality and safety for senior citizens. He shared his concern at the growing incidents of rape. 'It has obviously been a major concern for a long time, especially rapes, molestations and eve-teasing. It is very disrespectful to look at women in that way. It comes from the kind of society that we have built over the years where women have always been known to be treated as inferiors. How can this be done? This mentality is disturbing and needs to be condemned. If there was a culture of freedom and equality for everyone, these things would not have happened. People would have a fear of not judging anyone on gender. It is a question of equality and how we internalise this.' This was a new aspect of Virat's personality. Standing up for womens issues with a firm message.

He was not going to tolerate nonsense related to his personal life. As an icon, he realised the importance of the responsibility on his shoulders as the Indian cricket captain. 'The most difficult job in Indian sports,' was how once Pataudi had described the post. Virat was burdened with expectations and he chose to handle them with dignity. His commitment to cricket has not even left him with time to visit the Taj Mahal in Agra, or the Vaishno Devi Shrine in Jammu, two of his unfulfilled desires.

For some discerning observers, Virat's aggression had to do with his compelling urge to dominate, to win at any cost. 'He hates to lose,' remarked Dahiya. Who doesn't hate to lose? But Virat has been obsessed with winning. It helped Virat that he excelled in the T20 format that is essentially a game tailor-made for the new generation. 'Opening the innings has helped Virat a lot. He has learnt to express himself better and clearly with his wide range of shots. His consistency has been unheard of really and there is no failure with which to counter him. His penchant for big knocks complements his game,' said Dahiya.

Virat's impatience to excel is highly evident to his dressing room colleagues. Even as the openers pad up, he pads up too, never mind that he is listed to bat in the fourth position. He is ready in his battle gear even before a wicket has fallen. He wants to keep himself involved and once he is at the crease, Virat can change gears amazingly. He is a sprinter and a middle distance runner too. His game sense is phenomenal and he would not mind taking the back seat if his partner is on song. He is quick in deciding which bowler to attack and where to hit a certain bowler. Perfect execution.

What has made Virat a batsman to fear is his mind-blowing fitness coupled with strict diet control. He stopped eating wheat and rice, and worked on his physical and mental fitness. His ability to adapt is admirable. At the 2015 World Cup, he had admitted that hitting sixes was not his forte, but the same man was slamming sixes at the 2016 T20 World Cup and the IPL. What a transformation for the man whose calibre had been doubted by people when he made his debut. It was almost as if Virat forced his way into the hearts of cricket lovers, with that characteristic self-assertion. In comparison, someone like Unmukt made waves as a junior, but lost his momentum in the senior league.

Virat emerged successful as he went through the grind. Sehwag had failed on debut against Pakistan and developed insecurity against fast bowling. He was ousted by an express delivery from Shoaib Akhtar. He was to slay the same bowler a few years later after having worked on his game. Virat was not any different. 'What helped him was that he batted wherever the team management wanted him to. It is only now he is batting at No. 4, which is where he should bat ideally. He can also control the game at No. 3 because he is so confident of building the innings around him,' noted Dahiya.

Ganguly and Dhoni had nurtured their teams. Now Virat has the responsibility and opportunity to raise his army. As Dahiya said, 'It helps when he learns from mistakes. That is the key to his success because he can turn things around even when he is not at the peak. He knows his zone. He knows his best and weak points. I have seen from up close, the considerable change in his game and personality. Coming from North, it was natural that Virat was aggressive and flamboyant, but discipline was part of his personality and the game he played. He was never impulsive. He would calculate and then take charge. His determination to stick to his strict diet regimen is amazing. I remember his last Ranji match (against Uttar Pradesh in 2013). I did not see him at the food table when others were flocking to it. Such was his resolve,' said Dahiya.

Virat's involvement with the game won Dahiya's respect. 'We were playing a Ranji trophy match at the Roshanara Club. He was the captain. I had barely reached home after the pre-match practice when he called to ask me what was on my mind, what combination we could try, who could be the final eleven. I realised he had the necessary leadership qualities in him. This guy was thinking about the match when others were just resting after a tiring nets session. He was in a different league and I knew this cricketer was going to make it big.'

Having set the bar high, with nearly 1,000 runs in the 2016 IPL, Virat would still face tremendous pressure if he ran into a lean patch. For his fans, even a total of 600 runs in the 2017 IPL would amount to loss of form, such are the expectations from Virat. Comparisons have been drawn between Tendulkar and Virat which the latter has many times dismissed summarily. 'Please don't compare Sachin with Virat,' pleaded Sehwag. What about Virat and Sehwag? In spite of their aggressive batting, the two are temperamentally very different from each other. The major difference is in their body language. Sehwag was laid back and his understanding of the game was individualistic. He played to his strength and possessed a remarkable hand-eye co-ordination. Sehwag was mentally strong and silenced everyone with his daring batsmanship. He would look to hit a six even when on ninety-nine, 199, or 299. When Sehwag batted, the bowlers defended themselves. Virat too has learnt to utilise this talent and read the game differently. His consistency is superior to the likes of Sehwag, Richards and Gilchrist – all of them merciless belters of the ball.

Virat is also difficult to please. Bhatia was quite forthcoming when he remarked, 'Virat is rarely satisfied. It is a good sign, but then it multiplies the pressure on him. He wants to dominate in every situation and that is not always possible. He is yet to face a bad patch, even when he does; I know he will find ways to counter it. He has begun to mould his cricket, his batting, and his approach. He is beginning to look like a leader, even though he continues to stoke his desire to be the man of the moment always. He is still young as a captain, but tough, and needs to learn a lot,' assessed Bhatia.

His Delhi coach Chetan Chauhan, also his manager on a few tours overseas, never doubted Virat's ability to play big cricket with ease. 'I loved his passion. He will give everything he's got. How many would do what he did? His father's body was lying at home and he came to serve the team in a difficult situation. He went up in everyone's esteem that day and I have never failed to miss his batting since then. He is a man of strong character and would do wonders if he learnt to control his temper. He has an insatiable appetite for runs, higher than Tendulkar's. A sign of a great player is when he adjusts his game. Virat has done it. Just as Gavaskar did it. Gavaskar was a compulsive puller and hooker of the ball, but he gave it up when he discovered that he was giving away his wicket cheaply in wanting to assert his presence at the crease. Gavaskar became solid and consistent with time. Virat is in the same frame now.'

An aspect of his batting that has helped Virat grow is the comfort with which he picks the gaps. He can find gaps at will, which leads him to score more boundaries than sixes. It comes from the power that he packs into his shots, as well as the fact that he also knows the best way to pick up runs is to place the ball between the fielders. He is constantly analysing his game at the crease and evolving as a cricketer. It is tough to bowl to him because he has such a vast range of shots to play. The same ball can be driven through the cover, or just graze past cover-point, or savagely square cut. Virat is a phenomenon few bowlers can control or tame.

Virat is the most sought after youth icon today. A big hit on social media, he has found various means to interact with his fans. He promotes other games with an enthusiasm that is rare, be it kabaddi, hockey, football and futsal; apart from endorsing food products and cars. The most popular brand ambassador in India, he is among the richest sportsmen in the world. Virat Kohli has indeed come a long way from the day when he reported at Raj Kumar Sharma's academy to learn cricket. Today, the world is taking lessons from him.

Virat Kohli in Facts and Figures

Rajneesh Gupta

Full name: Virat Kohli

Born: 5 November 1988, Delhi

Style: Right-handed batsman & right-arm medium bowler

Teams: Delhi U-15s, Delhi U-17s, Delhi U-19s, Delhi, India U-19s, North Zone U-19s, India Red, North Zone, Royal Challengers Bangalore, National Cricket Academy, Indians, India, India A, Rest of India, Indian Board President's XI, Oil and Natural Gas Corporation

First-class debut: Delhi v Tamil Nadu at Delhi, 23 November 2006 (made 10 in only innings)

Highest first-class score: 197 (410 mins, 274 balls, 29 fours, 1 six), Delhi v Sui Northern Gas Pipes Limited at Delhi in September 2008.

Best first-class bowling (innings): 1-19 for Delhi v Bengal at Delhi in November 2010

Best first-class bowling (match): 2-42 for Delhi v Bengal at Delhi in November 2010

Test debut: v West Indies at Kingston, 20 June 2011 (made 4 & 15)

Test captaincy record: Played 10, Won 5, Lost 2, Drawn 3

FIRST-CLASS CAREER

Batting and Fielding

Type	Mts	Inns	NO	Runs	Hs	Avg	SR	100	50	0	4s	6s	Ct
Test	41	72	4	2994	169	44.02	52.92	11	12	4	352	9	36
Ranji Trophy	23	36	5	1574	173	50.77	54.50	5	5	2	216	10	24
Duleep Trophy	2	1	0	56	56	56.00	100.00	0	1	0	10	0	0
Irani Trophy	2	4	1	139	90	46.33	76.79	0	1	0	21	0	2
'A' Test	3	3	0	110	49	36.66	45.45	0	0	0	10	3	3
Other	2	4	1	370	197	123.33	69.02	2	1	0	56	2	2
TOTAL	73	120	11	5243	197	48.10	54.84	18	20	6	665	24	67

Bowling

Type	Mts	Balls	Runs	Wkts	Best	Avg	RPO	5WI	10WM
Test	41	150	70	0	–	–	2.80	0	0
Ranji Trophy	23	396	182	3	1–19	60.66	2.75	0	0
Duleep Trophy	2	72	72	0	–	–	6.00	0	0
Irani Trophy	2	–	–	–	–	–	–	–	–
'A' Test	3	–	–	–	–	–	–	–	–
Other	2	–	–	–	–	–	–	–	–
TOTAL	73	618	324	3	1–19	108.00	3.14	0	0

List A debut: For Delhi v Services at Delhi, 18 February 2006 (Ranji One-Day Trophy)

Highest List A score: 183 (148 balls, 22 fours, 1 six) for India v Pakistan at Mirpur, 18 March 2012 (One-Day International)

Best List A bowling: 1-15 for India v South Africa at Johannesburg, 12 December 2013 (One-Day International)

ODI debut: v Sri Lanka at Dambulla, 18 August 2008 (made 12 off 22 balls)

Highest ODI score: 183 (148 balls, 22 fours, 1 six) v Pakistan at Mirpur, 18 March 2012

Best ODI bowling: 1-15 v South Africa at Johannesburg, 5 December 2013

ODI captaincy record: Played 17, Won 14, Lost 3

LIST A CAREER

Batting and Fielding

Type	Mts	Inns	NO	Runs	Hs	Avg	SR	100	50	0	4s	6s	Ct
One-Day Internationals	171	163	23	7212	183	51.51	89.97	25	36	10	673	72	83
Vijay Hazare Trophy	14	13	1	819	124	68.25	106.08	4	3	0	91	17	2
Deodhar Trophy	7	7	1	281	79*	46.83	85.15	0	3	0	39	1	7
Challenger Series	11	11	1	248	63	24.80	79.74	0	1	1	24	5	8
Other	2	2	0	94	71	47.00	76.42	0	1	0	10	1	1
TOTAL	205	196	26	8654	183	50.90	90.59	29	44	11	837	96	101

Bowling

Type	Mts	Balls	Runs	Wkts	Best	Avg	RPO	4W
One-Day Internationals	171	611	636	4	1–15	159.00	6.24	0
Vijay Hazare Trophy	14	13	21	0	–	–	9.69	0
Deodhar Trophy	7	12	13	0	–	–	6.50	0
Challenger Series	11	39	27	0	–	–	4.15	0
Other	2	–	–	–	–	–	–	0
TOTAL	205	675	697	4	1–15	174.25	6.19	0

Twenty20 debut: For Delhi v Himachal Pradesh at Delhi, 3 April 2007 (Inter-State Twenty20 Tournament)

Highest Twenty20 score: 113 for Royal Challengers Bangalore v Kings XI Punjab at Bangalore, 18 May 2016 (IPL)

Best Twenty20 bowling: 2-25 for Royal Challengers Bangalore v Deccan Chargers at Hyderabad, 25 May 2008 (IPL)

T20I debut: v Zimbabwe at Harare, 12 June 2010 (made 26* off 21 balls)

Highest T20I score: 90* (55 balls, 9 fours, 2 sixes) v Australia at Adelaide, 26 January 2016

Best T20I bowling: 1-13 v England at Kolkata, 29 October 2011

T20I captaincy record: Yet to captain

TWENTY20 CAREER

Batting and Fielding

Type	Mts	Inns	NO	Runs	Hs	Avg	SR	100	50	0	4s	6s	Ct
Twenty20 Internationals	43	40	12	1641	90*	58.60	135.17	0	16	0	173	32	20
Indian Premier League	139	131	23	4110	113	38.05	130.43	4	26	5	359	148	55
Syed Mushtaq Ali Trophy	5	5	0	179	76	35.80	131.61	0	1	0	17	3	3
Champions League	15	14	3	424	84*	38.54	150.35	0	2	1	45	14	10
Other	2	2	0	91	78	45.50	144.44	0	1	0	8	3	1
TOTAL	204	192	38	6445	113	41.85	132.99	4	46	6	602	200	89

Bowling

Type	Mts	Balls	Runs	Wkts	Best	Avg	RPO	3W
Twenty20 Internationals	43	146	198	4	1–13	49.50	8.13	0
Indian Premier League	139	251	368	4	2–25	92.00	8.79	0
Syed Mushtaq Ali Trophy	5	–	–	–	–	–	–	–
Champions League	15	57	95	0	–	–	10.00	0
Other	2	–	–	–	–	–	–	–
TOTAL	204	454	661	8	2–25	82.62	8.73	0

VIRAT KOHLI IN TEST CRICKET
Performance in Each Match

Start Date	Against	Venue	Batting	Bowling	Fielding
20-06-2011	West Indies	Kingston	4 & 15		2 ct
28-06-2011	West Indies	Bridgetown	0 & 27		2 ct
06-07-2011	West Indies	Roseau	30		1 ct
22-11-2011	West Indies	Mumbai	52 & 63	0-9	2 ct
26-12-2011	Australia	Melbourne	11 & 0		2 ct
03-01-2012	Australia	Sydney	23 & 9	0-23	
13-01-2012	Australia	Perth	44 & 75		1 ct
24-01-2012	Australia	Adelaide	116 & 22	0-3	
23-08-2012	New Zealand	Hyderabad	58		4 ct
31-08-2012	New Zealand	Bangalore	103 & 51*		
15-11-2012	England	Ahmedabad	19 & 14*	.	1 ct
23-11-2012	England	Mumbai WS	19 & 7		1 ct
05-12-2012	England	Kolkata	6 & 20		
13-12-2012	England	Nagpur	103		2 ct
22-02-2013	Australia	Chennai	107		1 ct
02-03-2013	Australia	Hyderabad	34		1 ct
14-03-2013	Australia	Mohali	67* & 34		1 ct
22-03-2013	Australia	Delhi	1 & 41		2 ct
06-11-2013	West Indies	Kolkata	3		1 ct
14-11-2013	West Indies	Mumbai	57		
18-12-2013	South Africa	Johannesburg	119 & 96	dnb & 0-18	
26-12-2013	South Africa	Durban	46 & 11		1 ct
06-02-2014	New Zealand	Auckland	4 & 67	0-4	1 ct
14-02-2014	New Zealand	Wellington	38 & 105*	dnb & 0-13	1 ct
09-07-2014	England	Nottingham	1 & 8		
17-07-2014	England	Lord's	25 & 0		

Start Date	Against	Venue	Batting	Bowling	Fielding
27-07-2014	England	Southampton	39 & 28		
07-08-2014	England	Manchester	0 & 7		
15-08-2014	England	The Oval	6 & 20		1 ct
09-12-2014	Australia	Adelaide	115 & 141		1 ct
17-12-2014	Australia	Brisbane	19 & 1		1 ct
26-12-2014	Australia	Melbourne	169 & 54		
06-01-2015	Australia	Sydney	147 & 46		
10-06-2015	Bangladesh	Fatullah	14		
12-08-2015	Sri Lanka	Galle	103 & 3		
20-08-2015	Sri Lanka	Colombo PSS	78 & 10		1 ct
28-08-2015	Sri Lanka	Colombo SSC	18 & 21		2 ct
05-11-2015	South Africa	Mohali	1 & 29		1 ct
14-11-2015	South Africa	Bangalore	dnb		
25-11-2015	South Africa	Nagpur	22 & 16		2 ct
03-12-2015	South Africa	Delhi	44 & 88	dnb & 0-0	

dnb = did not bat / bowl

Innings Break-up

Runs	Innings
0	4
1-9	14
10-19	11
20-29	10
30-39	5
40-49	5
50-89	11
90-99	1
100-149	10
150+	1

Mode of Dismissals

	Innings
caught in the field	32
caught by keeper	19
bowled	4
leg before wicket	12
run out	1
Completed innings	68
(not out)	4

Pattern of Scoring

	Balls	Percentage
Dot balls	4111	72.67
1s	907	16.03
2s	209	3.69
3s	69	1.22
4s	352	6.22
5s	0	0.00
6s	9	0.16
Balls faced	5657	100.00

Performance against Each Country

	Mts	Inns	NO	Runs	Hs	Avg	SR	100	50	0	4s	6s
v Australia	12	22	1	1276	169	60.76	57.27	6	3	1	146	4
v Bangladesh	1	1	0	14	14	14.00	63.63	0	0	0	2	0
v England	9	17	1	322	103	20.12	39.12	1	0	2	40	0
v New Zealand	4	7	2	426	105*	85.20	58.75	2	3	0	63	2
v South Africa	6	10	0	472	119	47.20	53.94	1	2	0	58	0
v Sri Lanka	3	6	0	233	103	38.83	51.77	1	1	0	24	1
v West Indies	6	9	0	251	63	27.88	47.00	0	3	1	19	2
TOTAL	41	72	4	2994	169	44.02	52.92	11	12	4	352	9

Performance in Each Country

	Mts	Inns	NO	Runs	Hs	Avg	SR	100	50	0	4s	6s
in Australia	8	16	0	992	169	62.00	59.33	5	2	1	111	2
in Bangladesh	1	1	0	14	14	14.00	63.63	0	0	0	2	0
in England	5	10	0	134	39	13.40	46.52	0	0	2	15	0
in India	17	26	3	1059	107	46.04	48.84	3	7	0	129	4
in New Zealand	2	4	1	214	105*	71.33	62.39	1	1	0	32	1
in South Africa	2	4	0	272	119	68.00	55.73	1	1	0	33	0
in Sri Lanka	3	6	0	233	103	38.83	51.77	1	1	0	24	1
in West Indies	3	5	0	76	30	15.20	33.62	0	0	1	6	1
TOTAL	41	72	4	2994	169	44.02	52.92	11	12	4	352	9

	Mts	Inns	NO	Runs	Hs	Avg	SR	100	50	0	4s	6s
Home	17	26	3	1059	107	46.04	48.84	3	7	0	129	4
Away	24	46	1	1935	169	43.00	55.46	8	5	4	223	5
TOTAL	41	72	4	2994	169	44.02	52.92	11	12	4	352	9

Performance in Each Calendar Year

Year	Mts	Inns	NO	Runs	Hs	Avg	SR	100	50	0	4s	6s
2011	5	9	0	202	63	22.44	42.70	0	2	2	15	2
2012	9	16	2	689	116	49.21	46.74	3	3	0	89	2
2013	8	12	1	616	119	56.00	54.65	2	3	0	73	2
2014	10	20	1	847	169	44.57	60.54	4	2	2	101	2
2015	9	15	0	640	147	42.66	54.05	2	2	0	74	1
TOTAL	41	72	4	2994	169	44.02	52.92	11	12	4	352	9

Performance in Each Position

	Mts	Inns	NO	Runs	Hs	Avg	SR	100	50	0	4s	6s
3rd position	3	4	1	90	41	30.00	60.00	0	0	0	13	0
4th position	20	36	1	1630	169	46.57	58.15	7	4	2	194	3
5th position	17	22	2	859	107	42.95	45.21	3	5	1	103	4
6th position	5	9	0	404	116	44.88	51.59	1	3	1	41	2
7th position	1	1	0	11	11	11.00	52.38	0	0	0	1	0

Performance as Player / Captain

	Mts	Inns	NO	Runs	Hs	Avg	SR	100	50	0	4s	6s
as a player	31	55	4	2098	169	41.13	50.99	7	10	4	250	7
as a captain	10	17	0	896	147	52.70	58.06	4	2	0	102	2

Performance in Each Match Innings

	Mts	Inns	NO	Runs	Hs	Avg	SR	100	50	0	4s	6s
1st match innings	21	21	0	566	119	26.95	53.70	1	2	2	76	1
2nd match innings	20	19	1	1299	169	72.16	52.76	8	3	0	143	4
3rd match innings	18	18	0	460	96	25.55	43.07	0	3	1	50	1
4th match innings	16	14	3	669	141	60.81	62.34	2	4	1	83	3

	Mts	Inns	NO	Runs	Hs	Avg	SR	100	50	0	4s	6s
1st team innings	41	40	1	1865	169	47.82	53.04	9	5	2	219	5
2nd team innings	34	32	3	1129	141	38.93	52.73	2	7	2	133	4

Performance in Won / Lost / Drawn Matches

	Mts	Inns	NO	Runs	Hs	Avg	SR	100	50	0	4s	6s
in WON matches	16	27	3	960	107	40.00	52.06	2	6	1	122	4
in LOST matches	14	28	0	962	141	34.35	54.22	4	2	2	111	2
in DRAWN matches	11	17	1	1072	169	67.00	52.57	5	4	1	119	3

Notes:

- Made 44 and 75 in the Perth Test against Australia in January 2012 to become the third youngest Indian to top-score in both innings of a Test after Sunil Gavaskar and Lala Amarnath.

- Scored his maiden Test hundred at Adelaide against Australia in January 2012 at the age of 23 years 82 days. Only Sachin Tendulkar (18 years 256 days) and Dattu Phadkar (22 years 46 days) had scored a hundred for India on Australian soil at a younger age.

- Became only the fourth Indian to score a hundred on captaincy debut after Sunil Gavaskar, Dilip Vengsarkar and Vijay Hazare, when he notched up 115 against Australia at Adelaide in December 2014.

- By making 141 in the second innings of the above Adelaide Test, Virat became the only second player in Test chronicles to score hundreds in both innings of a Test on captaincy debut after Australia's Greg Chappell.

Hundred in both Innings on Captaincy Debut

Player	Scores	Opponent	Venue	Season
GS Chappell (Aus)	123 & 109*	West Indies	Brisbane	1975-76
V Kohli (Ind)	115 & 141	Australia	Adelaide	2014-15

Indian Players Scoring a Hundred on Captaincy Debut

Captain	Runs	Opponent	Venue	Season
VS Hazare	164*	England	Delhi	1951-52
SM Gavaskar	116	New Zealand	Auckland	1975-76
DB Vengsarkar	102	West Indies	Delhi	1987-88
V Kohli	115 & 141	Australia	Adelaide	2014-15

- At 26 years 38 days, Virat became the youngest captain to score two hundreds in a Test, taking the record from Zimbabwe's Brendan Taylor.

Youngest Captains to Score Hundred in both Innings of a Test

Age	Player	Scores	Vs	Venue	Season
26 Yrs 38 Days	V Kohli (Ind)	115 & 141	Aus	Adelaide	2014-15
27 Yrs 73 Days	BRM Taylor (Zim)	171 & 102*	Ban	Harare	2013
27 Yrs 117 Days	GS Chappell (Aus)	123 & 109*	WI	Brisbane	1975-76
28 Yrs 269 Days	RB Simpson (Aus)	153 & 115	Pak	Karachi	1964-65
29 Yrs 176 Days	SM Gavaskar (Ind)	107 & 182*	WI	Kolkata	1978-79

- The twin-hundreds at Adelaide made Virat the first opposition captain to score hundreds in both innings of a Test in Australia.
- Virat's match-tally of 256 runs in Adelaide Test is the highest for a player captaining his side for the first time in a Test.

Most Runs on Captaincy Debut

Runs	Captain	Scores	Vs	Venue	Season
256	V Kohli (Ind)	115 & 141	Aus	Adelaide	2014-15
244	GT Dowling (NZ)	239 & 5	Ind	Christchurch	1967-68
232	GS Chappell (Aus)	123 & 109*	WI	Brisbane	1975-76
212	AN Cook (Eng)	173 & 39	Ban	Chittagong	2009-10
203	S Chanderpaul (WI)	203*	SA	Georgetown	2004-05

- Virat became only the fourth Indian to score hundreds in both innings of a Test, following the foot-steps of Vijay Hazare, Sunil Gavaskar and Rahul Dravid. Gavaskar – at Kolkata – was the only Indian captain to accomplish this feat, before Virat joined him.

Indian Batsmen Scoring Hundreds in both Innings of a Test

Player	Scores	Opponent	Venue	Season
VS Hazare	116 & 145	Australia	Adelaide	1947-48
SM Gavaskar	124 & 220	West Indies	Port-of-Spain	1970-71
SM Gavaskar	111 & 137	Pakistan	Karachi	1978-79
SM Gavaskar+	107 & 182*	West Indies	Kolkata	1978-79
R Dravid	190 & 103*	New Zealand	Hamilton	1998-99
R Dravid	110 & 135	Pakistan	Kolkata	2004-05
V Kohli+	115 & 141	Australia	Adelaide	2014-15

+ as captain

- Virat's 141 is the third highest score by an Indian in the fourth innings of a Test.

Highest Scores by Indian Batsmen in 4th Innings of a Test

Player	Runs	Opponent	Venue	Season
SM Gavaskar	221	England	The Oval	1979
DB Vengsarkar	146*	Pakistan	Delhi	1979-80
V Kohli	141	Australia	Adelaide	2014-15
SR Tendulkar	136	Pakistan	Chennai	1998-99
VS Hazare	122	West Indies	Mumbai BS	1948-49
Yuvraj Singh	122	Pakistan	Karachi	2005-06

- Virat is one of the four Indian batsmen to score a hundred in 4th innings of a Test more than once – after Sunil Gavaskar (4), Sachin Tendulkar (3) and Mohammad Azharuddin (2).
- The innings of 147 at Sydney in the fourth and final Test of 2014-15 series against Australia gave Virat the unique distinction of scoring three hundreds in first three innings as Test captain.
- Virat's tally of 692 runs against Australia in 2014-15 is the third best by an Indian batsman in a series.

Indian Batsmen with Most Runs in a Series

Runs	Player	Series	Season	Mts	Avg	100s
774	SM Gavaskar	v WI in WI	1970-71	4	154.80	4
732	SM Gavaskar	v WI in Ind	1978-79	6	91.50	4
692	V Kohli	v Aus in Aus	2014-15	4	86.50	4
642	DN Sardesai	v WI in WI	1970-71	5	80.25	3
619	R Dravid	v Aus in Aus	2003-04	4	123.80	1
602	R Dravid	v Eng in Eng	2002	4	100.33	3

- Became first Indian captain to win an away series after losing the first Test. Virat did so against Sri Lanka in 2015 where India lost the first Test at Galle, but then bounced back by winning the consecutive Tests in Colombo. Even at home only two – Ajit Wadekar and Sourav Ganguly – have accomplished this feat.
- By winning the 2015 series against Sri Lanka 2-1, Virat Kohli became the youngest Indian captain to win a series outside India.

Youngest Indian Captains to Win an Away Test Series

Captain	Age	Series	Result
Virat Kohli	26 yrs 300 days	v Sri Lanka in Sri Lanka, 2015	2-1
MAK Pataudi	27 yrs 67 days	v New Zealand in NZ, 1967-68	3-1
Kapil Dev	27 yrs 168 days	v England in England, 1986	2-0
MS Dhoni	27 yrs 274 days	v New Zealand in NZ, 2008-09	2-0

- Only Indian captain to beat South Africa 3-0 in a Test series.
- Averages 52.71 as captain in Tests (896 runs in 10 matches with 4 hundreds) – the highest by an Indian captain.

- Virat's average of 60.81 in the fourth innings of Tests is the second highest for an Indian batsman having batted on 10 or more occasions.
- In 41 Tests Virat has scored 11 hundreds. Among all Indian batsmen only one – Sunil Gavaskar – had scored more hundreds (17) in first 41 Tests, while Virender Sehwag had also scored 11 hundreds in first 41 Tests.
- Virat Kohli has crossed fifty 23 times in his Test career and on 10 occasions he has gone on to score a hundred. Virat's conversion rate of 47.83 is the joint-second highest for an Indian with 10 or more hundreds, behind only Mohammad Azharuddin.

Highest 50 to 100 Conversion Rate for Indian Batsmen (Qual: 10 hundreds)

%	Player	No.of Times Crossed 50	100s scored
51.16	MA Azharuddin	43	22
47.83	RJ Shastri	23	11
47.83	V Kohli	23	11
46.15	PR Umrigar	26	12
43.04	SM Gavaskar	79	34
42.86	SR Tendulkar	119	51
42.59	V Sehwag	54	23

VIRAT KOHLI IN ONE-DAY INTERNATIONALS
Performance in Each Match

Date	Against	Venue	Batting	Bowling	Fielding
18-08-2008	Sri Lanka	Dambulla	12 (22)		
20-08-2008	Sri Lanka	Dambulla	37 (67)		3 ct
24-08-2008	Sri Lanka	Colombo RPS	25 (38)		
27-08-2008	Sri Lanka	Colombo RPS	54 (66)		
29-08-2008	Sri Lanka	Colombo RPS	31 (46)		
14-09-2009	Sri Lanka	Colombo RPS	2* (2)		
26-09-2009	Pakistan	Centurion	16 (24)	0-21 (3)	1 ct
28-09-2009	Australia	Centurion			
30-09-2009	West Indies	Johannesburg	79* (104)		
25-10-2009	Australia	Vadodara	30 (41)		1 ct
02-11-2009	Australia	Mohali	10 (16)		
15-12-2009	Sri Lanka	Rajkot	27 (19)		
18-12-2009	Sri Lanka	Nagpur	54 (65)		1 ct
24-12-2009	Sri Lanka	Kolkata	107 (114)		1 ct
27-12-2009	Sri Lanka	Delhi			
05-01-2010	Sri Lanka	Mirpur	9 (12)		
07-01-2010	Bangladesh	Mirpur	91 (102)		1 ct
10-01-2010	Sri Lanka	Mirpur	71* (68)		1 ct
11-01-2010	Bangladesh	Mirpur	102* (95)		1 ct
13-01-2010	Sri Lanka	Mirpur	2 (8)	0-12 (1.4)	1 ct
21-02-2010	South Africa	Jaipur	31 (46)		1 ct
24-02-2010	South Africa	Gwalior			
27-02-2010	South Africa	Ahmedabad	57 (71)	0-11 (2)	
28-05-2010	Zimbabwe	Bulawayo	0 (0)		
30-05-2010	Sri Lanka	Bulawayo	82 (92)		
03-06-2010	Zimbabwe	Harare	18 (29)		1 ct
05-06-2010	Sri Lanka	Harare	68 (95)		1 ct
16-06-2010	Bangladesh	Dambulla	11 (22)		
19-06-2010	Pakistan	Dambulla	18 (27)		1 ct
22-06-2010	Sri Lanka	Dambulla	10 (14)		
24-06-2010	Sri Lanka	Dambulla	28 (34)	0-16 (3)	
16-08-2010	Sri Lanka	Dambulla	0 (3)		

Date	Against	Venue	Batting	Bowling	Fielding
25-08-2010	New Zealand	Dambulla	8 (16)		
28-08-2010	Sri Lanka	Dambulla	37 (57)		
20-10-2010	Australia	Visakhapatnam	118 (121)		
28-11-2010	New Zealand	Guwahati	105 (104)		
01-12-2010	New Zealand	Jaipur	64 (73)		1 ct
04-12-2010	New Zealand	Vadodara	63* (70)		
07-12-2010	New Zealand	Bangalore	0 (2)		
10-12-2010	New Zealand	Chennai	2 (8)		
12-01-2011	South Africa	Durban	54 (70)		
15-01-2011	South Africa	Johannesburg	22 (34)		
18-01-2011	South Africa	Cape Town	28 (41)		3 ct
21-01-2011	South Africa	Port Elizabeth	87* (92)		1 ct
23-01-2011	South Africa	Centurion	2 (6)		
19-02-2011	Bangladesh	Mirpur	100* (83)		
27-02-2011	England	Bangalore	8 (5)		1 ct
06-03-2011	Ireland	Bangalore	34 (53)		
09-03-2011	Netherlands	Delhi	12 (20)		
12-03-2011	South Africa	Nagpur	1 (3)		1 ct
20-03-2011	West Indies	Chennai	59 (76)		
24-03-2011	Australia	Ahmedabad	24 (33)	0-6 (1)	
30-03-2011	Pakistan	Mohali	9 (21)		1 ct
02-04-2011	Sri Lanka	Mumbai WS	35 (49)	0-6 (1)	
06-06-2011	West Indies	Port-of-Spain	2 (8)	0-16 (3)	1 ct
08-06-2011	West Indies	Port-of-Spain	81 (103)		
11-06-2011	West Indies	North Sound	0 (1)	0-7 (1)	1 ct
13-06-2011	West Indies	North Sound	22 (33)		2 ct
16-06-2011	West Indies	Kingston	94 (104)	0-13 (3)	
03-09-2011	England	Chester-le-Street	55 (73)		
06-09-2011	England	Southampton	9 (9)	0-22 (3)	2 ct
09-09-2011	England	The Oval	7 (18)		
11-09-2011	England	Lord's	16 (36)		1 ct
16-09-2011	England	Cardiff	107 (93)	1-44 (6)	
14-10-2011	England	Hyderabad	37 (63)	0-11 (3)	
17-10-2011	England	Delhi	112* (98)	0-18 (5)	2 ct
20-10-2011	England	Mohali	35 (30)	1-20 (3)	

Date	Against	Venue	Batting	Bowling	Fielding
23-10-2011	England	Mumbai WS	86* (99)	0-14 (4)	1 ct
25-10-2011	England	Kolkata	0 (5)		1 ct
29-11-2011	West Indies	Cuttack	3 (6)		1 ct
02-12-2011	West Indies	Visakhapatnam	117 (123)		
05-12-2011	West Indies	Ahmedabad	20 (30)		
08-12-2011	West Indies	Indore	23* (11)		
11-12-2011	West Indies	Chennai	80 (85)	0-11 (1)	
05-02-2012	Australia	Melbourne	31 (34)	0-4 (1)	1 ct
08-02-2012	Sri Lanka	Perth	77 (94)		1 ct
12-02-2012	Australia	Adelaide	18 (28)		1 ct
14-02-2012	Sri Lanka	Adelaide	15 (25)		1 ct
19-02-2012	Australia	Brisbane	12 (25)		1 ct
21-02-2012	Sri Lanka	Brisbane	66 (83)	0-14 (1)	
26-02-2012	Australia	Sydney	21 (27)		1 ct
28-02-2012	Sri Lanka	Hobart	133* (86)		
13-03-2012	Sri Lanka	Mirpur	108 (120)		2 ct
16-03-2012	Bangladesh	Mirpur	66 (82)		
18-03-2012	Pakistan	Mirpur	183 (148)		2 ct
21-07-2012	Sri Lanka	Hambantota	106 (113)		1 ct
24-07-2012	Sri Lanka	Hambantota	1 (5)		
28-07-2012	Sri Lanka	Colombo RPS	38 (65)		1 ct
31-07-2012	Sri Lanka	Colombo RPS	128* (119)	0-7 (2)	1 ct
04-08-2012	Sri Lanka	Pallekele	23 (35)	0-3 (1)	1 ct
30-12-2012	Pakistan	Chennai	0 (5)	0-21 (2.5)	
03-01-2013	Pakistan	Kolkata	6 (9)		
06-01-2013	Pakistan	Delhi	7 (17)		
11-01-2013	England	Rajkot	15 (22)	0-9 (1)	1 ct
15-01-2013	England	Kochi	37 (54)		
19-01-2013	England	Ranchi	77* (79)		
23-01-2013	England	Mohali	26 (33)		
27-01-2013	England	Dharamsala	0 (1)		
06-06-2013	South Africa	Cardiff	31 (41)		
11-06-2013	West Indies	The Oval	22 (18)	0-26 (4)	
15-06-2013	Pakistan	Birmingham	22* (27)	0-11 (2)	1 ct
20-06-2013	Sri Lanka	Cardiff	58* (64)		

Date	Against	Venue	Batting	Bowling	Fielding
23-06-2013	England	Birmingham	43 (34)		
30-06-2013	West Indies	Kingston	11 (21)		
02-07-2013	Sri Lanka	Kingston	2 (5)	0-9 (2)	
05-07-2013	West Indies	Port-of-Spain	102 (83)		
09-07-2013	Sri Lanka	Port-of-Spain	31 (52)		1 ct
11-07-2013	Sri Lanka	Port-of-Spain	2 (5)	0-17 (3)	
24-07-2013	Zimbabwe	Harare	115 (108)		
26-07-2013	Zimbabwe	Harare	14 (18)		
28-07-2013	Zimbabwe	Harare	68* (88)	0-7 (1)	
01-08-2013	Zimbabwe	Bulawayo			1 ct
03-08-2013	Zimbabwe	Bulawayo			2 ct
13-10-2013	Australia	Pune	61 (85)	0-12 (1)	1 ct
16-10-2013	Australia	Jaipur	100* (52)		
19-10-2013	Australia	Mohali	68 (73)	0-18 (1)	
23-10-2013	Australia	Ranchi			
30-10-2013	Australia	Nagpur	115* (66)	0-15 (2)	2 ct
02-11-2013	Australia	Bangalore	0 (3)		1 ct
21-11-2013	West Indies	Kochi	86 (84)		
24-11-2013	West Indies	Visakhapatnam	99 (100)		
27-11-2013	West Indies	Kanpur	19 (18)		
05-12-2013	South Africa	Johannesburg	31 (35)	1-15 (2)	1 ct
08-12-2013	South Africa	Durban	0 (5)	0-17 (3)	
11-12-2013	South Africa	Centurion		0-22 (3)	
19-01-2014	New Zealand	Napier	123 (111)	0-13 (3)	
22-01-2014	New Zealand	Hamilton	78 (65)	0-12 (2)	
25-01-2014	New Zealand	Auckland	6 (20)		
28-01-2014	New Zealand	Hamilton	2 (10)		
31-01-2014	New Zealand	Wellington	82 (78)	1-36 (7)	
26-02-2014	Bangladesh	Fatullah	136 (122)	0-6 (1.1)	
28-02-2014	Sri Lanka	Fatullah	48 (51)		
02-03-2014	Pakistan	Mirpur	5 (11)		
05-03-2014	Afghanistan	Mirpur			2 ct
27-08-2014	England	Cardiff	0 (3)		1 ct
30-08-2014	England	Nottingham	40 (50)		
02-09-2014	England	Birmingham	1* (3)		

Date	Against	Venue	Batting	Bowling	Fielding
05-09-2014	England	Leeds	13 (21)		
08-10-2014	West Indies	Kochi	2 (5)		1 ct
11-10-2014	West Indies	Delhi	62 (78)	0-20 (2)	1 ct
17-10-2014	West Indies	Dharamsala	127 (114)	0-14 (1)	
02-11-2014	Sri Lanka	Cuttack	22 (21)	0-6 (0.5)	1 ct
06-11-2014	Sri Lanka	Ahmedabad	49 (44)		
09-11-2014	Sri Lanka	Hyderabad	53 (61)		1 ct
13-11-2014	Sri Lanka	Kolkata	66 (64)		1 ct
16-11-2014	Sri Lanka	Ranchi	139* (126)		
18-01-2015	Australia	Melbourne	9 (16)		
20-01-2015	England	Brisbane	4 (8)		1 ct
26-01-2015	Australia	Sydney	3* (9)		
30-01-2015	England	Perth	8 (19)		
15-02-2015	Pakistan	Adelaide	107 (126)		1 ct
22-02-2015	South Africa	Melbourne	46 (60)		1 ct
28-02-2015	U.A.E.	Perth	33* (41)		
06-03-2015	West Indies	Perth	33 (36)		2 ct
10-03-2015	Ireland	Hamilton	44* (42)		
14-03-2015	Zimbabwe	Auckland	38 (48)		
19-03-2015	Bangladesh	Melbourne	3 (8)		
26-03-2015	Australia	Sydney	1 (13)	0-7 (1)	1 ct
18-06-2015	Bangladesh	Mirpur	1 (4)	0-12 (2)	1 ct
21-06-2015	Bangladesh	Mirpur	23 (27)		
24-06-2015	Bangladesh	Mirpur	25 (35)		
11-10-2015	South Africa	Kanpur	11 (18)	0-1 (0.2)	
14-10-2015	South Africa	Indore	12 (18)		3 ct
18-10-2015	South Africa	Rajkot	77 (99)		
22-10-2015	South Africa	Chennai	138 (140)		
25-10-2015	South Africa	Mumbai WS	7 (6)	0-14 (2)	1 ct
12-01-2016	Australia	Perth	91 (97)	0-13 (2)	2 ct
15-01-2016	Australia	Brisbane	59 (67)	0-7 (1)	1 ct
17-01-2016	Australia	Melbourne	117 (117)		
20-01-2016	Australia	Canberra	106 (92)		1 ct
23-01-2016	Australia	Sydney	8 (11)		

Innings Break-up

Runs	Innings
0	10
1-9	32
10-19	19
20-29	17
30-39	18
40-49	6
50-89	32
90-99	4
100-149	24
150+	1

Mode of Dismissals

	Innings
caught in the field	67
caught by keeper	32
bowled	16
leg before wicket	11
run out	11
stumped	2
hit wicket	1
Completed innings	140
(not out)	23

Pattern of Scoring

	Balls	Percentage
Dot balls	3793	47.32
1s	2919	36.41
2s	517	6.45
3s	38	0.47
4s	674	8.41
5s	1	0.01
6s	74	0.92
Balls faced	8016	100.00

Performance against Each Country

	Mts	Inns	NO	Runs	Hs	Avg	SR	100	50	0	4s	6s
v Afghanistan	1	–	–	–	–	–	–	–	–	–	–	–
v Australia	23	21	3	1002	118	55.66	97.66	5	4	1	95	13
v Bangladesh	10	10	2	558	136	69.75	96.20	3	2	0	51	5
v England	23	23	4	736	112*	38.73	85.98	2	3	3	69	6
v Ireland	2	2	1	78	44*	78.00	82.10	0	0	0	7	1
v Netherlands	1	1	0	12	12	12.00	60.00	0	0	0	2	0
v New Zealand	11	11	1	533	123	53.30	95.69	2	4	1	51	9
v Pakistan	10	10	1	373	183	41.44	89.87	2	0	1	37	1
v South Africa	19	17	1	635	138	39.68	80.89	1	4	1	41	10
v Sri Lanka	40	39	6	1856	139*	56.24	88.00	6	10	1	173	14
v U.A.E.	1	1	1	33	33*	-	80.48	0	0	0	5	0
v West Indies	22	22	2	1143	127	57.15	92.10	3	8	1	117	11
v Zimbabwe	8	6	1	253	115	50.60	86.94	1	1	1	25	2
TOTAL	171	163	23	7212	183	51.51	89.97	25	36	10	673	72

Performance in Each Country

	Mts	Inns	NO	Runs	Hs	Avg	SR	100	50	0	4s	6s
in Australia	23	23	3	1001	133*	50.05	89.21	4	4	0	86	7
in Bangladesh	16	15	3	970	183	80.83	100.20	5	3	0	94	7
in England	14	14	3	424	107	38.54	86.53	1	2	1	35	4
in India	63	60	8	2844	139*	54.69	93.09	10	16	5	272	33
in New Zealand	7	7	1	373	123	62.16	99.73	1	2	0	34	8
in South Africa	11	9	2	319	87*	45.57	77.61	0	3	1	30	5
in Sri Lanka	18	18	2	569	128*	35.56	75.76	2	1	1	58	2
in West Indies	10	10	0	347	102	34.70	83.61	1	2	1	34	4
in Zimbabwe	9	7	1	365	115	60.83	84.88	1	3	1	30	2
TOTAL	171	163	23	7212	183	51.51	89.97	25	36	10	673	72

	Mts	Inns	NO	Runs	Hs	Avg	SR	100	50	0	4s	6s
Home	63	60	8	2844	139*	54.69	93.09	10	16	5	272	33
Away	72	69	8	2885	136	47.29	88.09	11	13	5	264	30
Neutral	36	34	7	1483	183	54.92	87.95	4	7	0	137	9
TOTAL	171	163	23	7212	183	51.51	89.97	25	36	10	673	72

Performance in each Calendar Year

Year	Mts	Inns	NO	Runs	Hs	Avg	SR	100	50	0	4s	6s
2008	5	5	0	159	54	31.80	66.52	0	1	0	21	1
2009	10	8	2	325	107	54.16	84.41	1	2	0	36	3
2010	25	24	3	995	118	47.38	85.11	3	7	3	90	4
2011	34	34	5	1381	117	47.62	85.56	4	8	2	127	7
2012	17	17	2	1026	183	68.40	93.78	5	3	1	92	5
2013	34	30	6	1268	115*	52.83	97.53	4	7	3	137	20
2014	21	20	2	1054	139*	58.55	99.62	4	5	1	94	20
2015	20	20	3	623	138	36.64	80.59	2	1	0	44	8
2016	5	5	0	381	117	76.20	99.21	2	2	0	32	4
TOTAL	171	163	23	7212	183	51.51	89.97	25	36	10	673	72

Performance in Each Position

	Mts	Inns	NO	Runs	Hs	Avg	SR	100	50	0	4s	6s
1st position	3	3	0	110	54	36.66	73.33	0	1	0	14	1
2nd position	3	3	0	51	37	17.00	51.51	0	0	0	7	0
3rd position	112	112	14	5123	183	52.27	90.72	18	26	10	475	57
4th position	37	37	7	1744	139*	58.13	90.40	7	8	0	161	14
5th position	3	3	0	123	80	41.00	81.45	0	1	0	8	0
6th position	1	1	1	23	23*	–	209.09	0	0	0	3	0
7th position	4	4	1	38	27	12.66	131.03	0	0	0	5	0
TOTAL	171	163	23	7212	183	51.51	89.97	25	36	10	673	72

Performance as Player / Captain

	Mts	Inns	NO	Runs	Hs	Avg	SR	100	50	0	4s	6s
as a player	154	149	21	6362	183	49.70	88.82	21	33	10	590	59
as a captain	17	14	2	850	139*	70.83	99.53	4	3	0	83	13
TOTAL	171	163	23	7212	183	51.51	89.97	25	36	10	673	72

Performance in Each Match Innings

	Mts	Inns	NO	Runs	Hs	Avg	SR	100	50	0	4s	6s
1st match innings	73	72	4	2804	138	41.23	86.40	10	14	6	233	21
2nd match innings	98	91	19	4408	183	61.22	92.39	15	22	4	440	51
TOTAL	171	163	23	7212	183	51.51	89.97	25	36	10	673	72

Performance in Won / Lost / Tied / No Result Matches

	Mts	Inns	NO	Runs	Hs	Avg	SR	100	50	0	4s	6s
in WON matches	99	95	21	4995	183	67.50	93.57	21	19	6	487	51
in LOST matches	62	62	1	2114	123	34.65	84.22	4	16	4	178	21
in TIED matches	4	4	0	45	16	11.25	52.32	0	0	0	4	0
in NO Result matches	6	2	1	58	55	58.00	70.73	0	1	0	4	0
TOTAL	171	163	23	7212	183	51.51	89.97	25	36	10	673	72

Notes:

- Fastest Indian cricketer to reach 1,000 runs in ODIs with Shikhar Dhawan (24 innings)
- Fastest Indian cricketer to reach 4,000 runs in ODIs (93 innings)
- Fastest Indian cricketer to reach 5,000 runs in ODIs (114 innings)
- Fastest Indian cricketer to reach 6,000 runs in ODIs (136 innings)
- Fastest cricketer to reach 7,000 runs in ODIs (161 innings)
- Fastest Indian cricketer to reach 10 centuries in ODIs
- Fastest Indian cricketer to reach 15 centuries in ODIs and second fastest overall behind Hashim Amla
- Fastest Indian cricketer to reach 20 centuries in ODIs and second fastest overall behind Hashim Amla
- Fastest cricketer to reach 25 centuries in ODIs
- Virat is one of the five batsmen with an average of 50 in a career of 100 ODIs or more. Michael Bevan, M.S. Dhoni, AB de Villiers and Hashim Amla are the others.
- Only Indian to score a hundred on World Cup debut (100* v Bangladesh, Mirpur, February 2011)
- Made 133* off 86 balls in India's mammoth chase of 321-3 in just 36.4 overs in a CB Series match against Sri Lanka at Hobart in February 2012.
- Virat's 183 at Mirpur in March 2012 is the highest innings by any batsman against Pakistan. It is also the joint second highest score by any batsman in a chase in ODIs.
- Scored four hundreds in five innings in 2012.
- In 2012 Virat aggregated 850 runs in 10 innings at an

average of 106.25 with 5 hundreds and 2 fifties between February and July. Virat's aggregate is the highest ever by any batsman in a span of 10 innings in One-Day Internationals, beating Australia's Matthew Hayden's previous record of 802 runs in 2007.

- In 2012 Virat raced to 1,000 run-mark in just 15 innings, equaling South Africa's Hashim Amla's record of taking fewest innings to complete 1,000 runs in a calendar year. Amla had done so in 2010.
- Led India for the first time in an ODI at the age of 24 years 239 days, having already appeared in 104 ODIs!
- Became the first Indian captain to win a bilateral ODI series 5-0 outside India – against Zimbabwe in August 2003.
- Virat's 52-ball hundred vs Australia at Jaipur in October 2013 is the fastest ODI hundred by an Indian, the fastest against Australia and third fastest in a chase.
- Reached the number one spot in the ICC rankings for ODI batsmen for the first time in 2013.
- Is the only Indian batsman to score two consecutive hundreds in ODIs on four occassions. In all ODIs, only AB de Villiers (6) has done so more often.
- Virat is one of the two batsmen to make five successive scores of 50 or more in ODIs on two separate occasions (New Zealand's Kane Williamson is the other).
- For five consecutive calendar years (2010, 2011, 2012, 2013 & 2104), Virat was India's leading run-scorer in ODIs, with 995, 1,381, 1,026, 1,268 and 1,054 runs respectively.
- Only the second player to aggregate 1,000 ODI runs for four consecutive years after Sourav Ganguly.
- Virat's ODI batting average of 61.22 is the highest in chases in ODIs for any batsman playing at least 25 innings.

- On an average Virat scores a hundred in every 6.52 innings, which is the best for an Indian and third best in all ODIs among batsmen with a minimum of 10 hundreds.

Virat's Hundreds in Chases

Score	SR	Target	Came in at	Dismissed at	Match	Result
107 (114)	93.85	316	23/2 (3.4)	247/3 (39.2)	v SL, Kolkata, 2009	Won-7 wkts
102* (95)	107.36	248	64/1 (11.5)	–	v Ban, Mirpur, 2010	Won-6 wkts
118 (121)	97.52	290	0/1 (0.2)	256/4 (43.2)	v Aus, Visakhapatnam, 2010	Won-5 wkts
112* (98)	114.28	238	29/2 (6.5)	–	v Eng, Delhi, 2011	Won-8 wkts
117 (123)	95.12	270	29/2 (6.4)	247/4 (44.6)	v WI, Visakhapatnam, 2011	Won-5 wkts
133* (86)	154.65	321	86/2 (9.2)	–	v SL, Hobart, 2012	Won-7 wkts
183 (148)	123.64	330	0/1 (0.2)	318/4 (47.1)	v Pak, Mirpur, 2012	Won-6 wkts
128* (119)	107.56	252	0/1 (0.5)	–	v SL, Colombo, 2012	Won-6 wkts
115 (108)	106.48	230	26/1 (6.3)	216/3 (41.3)	v Zim, Harare, 2013	Won-6 wkts
100* (52)	192.30	360	176/1 (26.1)	–	v Aus, Jaipur, 2013	Won-9 wkts
115* (66)	174.24	351	178/1 (29.3)	–	v Aus, Nagpur, 2013	Won-6 wkts
123 (111)	110.81	293	15/1 (5.2)	237/7 (44.2)	v NZ, Napier, 2014	Lost-24 runs
136 (122)	111.48	280	50/1 (11.2)	267/3 (45.4)	v Ban, Fatullah, 2014	Won-6 wkts
139* (126)	110.32	287	14/2 (4.3)	–	v SL, Ranchi, 2014	Won-3 wkts
106 (92)	115.22	349	65/1 (7.6)	278/4 (39.1)	v Aus, Canberra, 2016	Lost-25 runs

- Has scored 13 hundreds in successful chases in ODIs. Only Sachin Tendulkar – with 14 – is ahead.

- IIn all the 163 innings that he has batted in ODIS, Virat has been the top-scorer for India on 44 occasions – a percentage of 26.99. Among the Indians who have played at least 25 innings, only Sachin Tendulkar has the higher percentage – 28.54 (129 times top-scorer out of 452 innings).
- Among the Indians, only Sachin Tendulkar's rate of winning player of the match awards is better than Virat Kohli in ODIs.

Least Matches per Award in ODIs for India (Qual: 5 Awards)

	Matches	MoM awards	Match / Award
SR Tendulkar	463	62	7.47
V Kohli	171	21	8.14
SC Ganguly	311	31	10.03
NS Sidhu	136	13	10.46
V Sehwag	251	23	10.91
M Amarnath	85	8	10.63
Yuvraj Singh	293	25	11.72
G Gambhir	147	12	12.25
K Srikkanth	146	11	13.27
MS Dhoni	276	20	13.80

- Virat has been involved in eight double century partnerships in ODIs – a world record!
- Virat has captained India in 17 ODIs, winning 14 and losing only 3 – a win-percentage of 82.35. Among all players who have captained their respective teams in 10 matches or more, only one – Shane Warne (90.90) – has the higher win-percentage.

VIRAT KOHLI IN TWENTY20 INTERNATIONALS
Performance in Each Match

Date	Against	Venue	Batting	Bowling	Fielding
12-06-2010	Zimbabwe	Harare	26* (21)		
13-06-2010	Zimbabwe	Harare			
09-01-2011	South Africa	Durban	28 (19)		1 ct
04-06-2011	West Indies	Port-of-Spain	14 (12)		2 ct
31-08-2011	England	Manchester	4 (5)	1-22 (3)	
29-10-2011	England	Kolkata	15 (16)	1-13 (2.4)	
01-02-2012	Australia	Sydney	22 (21)		
03-02-2012	Australia	Melbourne	31 (24)	0-7 (1)	
30-03-2012	South Africa	Johannesburg		0-15 (1)	
07-08-2012	Sri Lanka	Pallekele	68 (48)	0-13 (3)	1 ct
11-09-2012	New Zealand	Chennai	70 (41)	0-27 (3)	
19-09-2012	Afghanistan	Colombo RPS	50 (39)		
23-09-2012	England	Colombo RPS	40 (32)		1 ct
28-09-2012	Australia	Colombo RPS	15 (13)	0-10 (1)	
30-09-2012	Pakistan	Colombo RPS	78* (61)	1-21 (3)	
02-10-2012	South Africa	Colombo RPS	2 (6)		
20-12-2012	England	Pune	21 (17)	0-10 (1)	1 ct
22-12-2012	England	Mumbai WS	38 (20)		
25-12-2012	Pakistan	Bangalore	9 (11)	0-21 (2)	
28-12-2012	Pakistan	Ahmedabad	27 (22)		2 ct
10-10-2013	Australia	Rajkot	29 (22)	0-24 (2)	
21-03-2014	Pakistan	Mirpur	36* (32)		
23-03-2014	West Indies	Mirpur	54 (41)		1 ct
28-03-2014	Bangladesh	Mirpur	57* (50)		1 ct
30-03-2014	Australia	Mirpur	23 (22)		2 ct
04-04-2014	South Africa	Mirpur	72* (44)		

Date	Against	Venue	Batting	Bowling	Fielding
06-04-2014	Sri Lanka	Mirpur	77 (58)		1 ct
07-09-2014	England	Birmingham	66 (41)		
02-10-2015	South Africa	Dharamsala	43 (27)		
05-10-2015	South Africa	Cuttack	1 (1)		
26-01-2016	Australia	Adelaide	90* (55)		2 ct
29-01-2016	Australia	Melbourne	59* (33)		
31-01-2016	Australia	Sydney	50 (36)		
24-02-2016	Bangladesh	Mirpur	7 (12)		
27-02-2016	Pakistan	Mirpur	49 (51)		
01-03-2016	Sri Lanka	Mirpur	56* (47)		
03-03-2016	U.A.E.	Mirpur			1 ct
06-03-2016	Bangladesh	Mirpur	41* (28)		1 ct
15-03-2016	New Zealand	Nagpur	23 (27)		
19-03-2016	Pakistan	Kolkata	55* (37)		1 ct
23-03-2016	Bangladesh	Bangalore	24 (24)		1 ct
27-03-2016	Australia	Mohali	82* (51)		1 ct
31-03-2016	West Indies	Mumbai WS	89* (47)	1-15 (1.4)	

Performance against Each Country

	Mts	Inns	NO	Runs	Hs	Avg	SR	100	50	0	4s	6s
v Afghanistan	1	1	0	50	50	50.00	128.20	0	1	0	4	2
v Australia	9	9	3	401	90*	66.83	144.76	0	4	0	36	9
v Bangladesh	4	4	2	129	57*	64.50	113.15	0	1	0	9	2
v England	6	6	0	184	66	30.66	140.45	0	1	0	27	1
v New Zealand	2	2	0	93	70	46.50	136.76	0	1	0	12	1
v Pakistan	6	6	3	254	78*	84.66	118.69	0	2	0	30	4
v South Africa	6	5	1	146	72*	36.50	150.51	0	1	0	11	5
v Sri Lanka	3	3	1	201	77	100.50	131.37	0	3	0	23	5
v U.A.E.	1	–	–	–	–	–	–	–	–	–	–	–
v West Indies	3	3	1	157	89*	78.50	157.00	0	2	0	18	2
v Zimbabwe	2	1	1	26	26*	–	123.80	0	0	0	3	1
TOTAL	43	40	12	1641	90*	58.60	135.17	0	16	0	173	32

Notes:

- Highest run-getter for India in Twenty20 Internationals with 1641 runs in 40 innings at an average of 58.61
- Has more fifty-plus scores than any other batsman – 16.
- Has the highest batting average among all batsmen who have played 5 innings or more.

Highest Batting Average in T20Is (Qual: 5 Innings)

	Mts	Inns	Runs	Avg	SR	100	50
V Kohli (Ind)	43	40	1641	58.60	135.17	0	16
ML Hayden (Aus)	9	9	308	51.33	143.92	0	4
HA Varaiya (Ken)	25	12	51	51.00	62.96	0	0
JM Kemp (SA)	8	7	203	50.75	126.87	0	1
A Symonds (Aus)	14	11	337	48.14	169.34	0	2
AC Voges (Aus)	7	5	139	46.33	121.92	0	1
NO Miller (WI)	9	5	43	43.00	91.48	0	0
RN ten Doeschate (Net)	9	9	214	42.80	128.91	0	1
N Vanua (PNG)	6	5	83	41.50	172.91	0	0
MW Machan (Scot)	13	13	407	40.70	127.98	0	3
A Bagai (Can)	9	9	284	40.57	114.05	0	2

- Has scored 918 runs in 19 chases at an average of 91.80 with 10 scores of fifty or more. Only one player – Brendon McCullum – has aggregated more runs in chases than Virat (88 more runs in 19 more innings).

Highest Run-Aggregate in Chases in T20Is

	Mts	Inns	Runs	Hs	Avg	SR	100	50
BB McCullum (NZ)	38	38	1006	81*	33.53	127.34	0	7
V Kohli (Ind)	22	19	918	82*	91.80	132.65	0	10
MJ Guptill (NZ)	33	31	882	101*	35.28	128.01	1	5
DA Warner (Aus)	34	34	867	77	27.09	142.83	0	7
SR Watson (Aus)	34	32	780	72	26.00	141.04	0	7
TM Dilshan (SL)	33	32	777	83*	31.08	120.46	0	7
AD Hales (Eng)	24	24	752	116*	37.60	139.00	1	5

- In successful chases Virat averages a mind-boggling 122.83 – easily the highest for any batsman.

Most Prolific Batsmen in Successful Chases in T20Is

	Mts	Inns	Runs	Hs	Avg	SR	100	50
V Kohli (Ind)	17	15	737	82*	122.83	131.13	0	8
MJ Guptill (NZ)	16	14	611	101*	76.37	139.81	1	5
SR Watson (Aus)	19	17	601	72	40.06	147.66	0	6
BB McCullum (NZ)	18	18	572	81*	57.20	136.84	0	5
CH Gayle (WI)	13	12	519	100*	47.18	177.13	1	4
DA Warner (Aus)	17	17	508	77	33.86	156.79	0	4

- Reached the number one spot in the ICC rankings for T20Is batsmen for the first time in 2014.
- In 2015, he became the fastest batsman in the world to 1,000 runs in T20Is (27 innings).
- In 2016, he became the fastest batsman in the world to 1,500 runs in T20Is (39 innings).
- Is the only player to have scored three consecutive fifties on three occasions.

- Virat's run-tally of 777 is the highest for any Indian batsman in World T20.
- In 2016 Virat has scored 625 runs in Twenty20 Internationals – most by any batsman in this format in a calendar year.
- Virat's tally of 319 runs in World T20 2014 is the highest for any batsman in a T20I tournament.
- 25.85% of runs scored by India in Twenty20 Internationals have come off Virat's bat – highest percentage for any player with five or more matches.
- In 43 matches, Virat has won player of the match award on nine occasions. Only Shahid Afridi has won more awards – 11 (he has played 55 more games than Virat). Three other players – Chris Gayle, Mohammad Shahzad and Shane Watson – have also same number of awards as Virat, but they have all played more matches.
- In 2016, Virat has won six player of the match awards – most by any player in a calendar year. Shane Watson had won five awards in 2012.
- Virat has won five player of the match awards in World T20 – most by any player, along with Chris Gayle, Mahela Jayawardene and Shane Watson. Virat has played fewest matches among the four.
- In 2016, Virat scored fifties in all matches of three-match series against Australia – most fifties by any batsman in a bilateral series.
- Virat has scored four consecutive fifties against Australia – 90*, 59*, 50 and 82*. This is the longest streak of fifty-plus scores for a batsman against any opponent in Twenty20 Internationals.
- Virat has aggregated 472 runs in 11 Twenty20 Internationals at Shere Bangla National Stadium,

Mirpur – most by any batsman at a particular ground in this format.

- Virat is yet to be dismissed for a duck in Twenty20 Internationals.
- Between 2012 and 2015, Virat scored at least 20 in 10 consecutive innings – a world record he shares with New Zealand's Kane Williamson.
- Man of the Tournament in ICC World T20, 2014 and 2016.
- Took a wicket off his first delivery in Twenty20 Internationals when he got England's Kevin Pietersen out stumped off a wide at Manchester in August 2011.

INDIAN PREMIER LEAGUE (IPL)

- First player to reach 4,000 run-mark in IPL.
- Highest run-aggregate in IPL with 4,110 runs (avg 38.06) in 139 matches

Most Runs in IPL

	Mts	Runs	Hs	Avg	SR	100	50
V Kohli	139	4110	113	38.06	130.43	4	26
SK Raina	147	4098	100*	33.59	138.59	1	28
RG Sharma	142	3874	109*	33.69	131.72	1	29
G Gambhir	132	3634	93	30.54	124.15	0	31
CH Gayle	92	3426	175*	43.37	153.29	5	20
RV Uthappa	135	3390	83*	29.48	128.65	0	17
DA Warner	100	3373	109*	38.33	142.20	2	32
MS Dhoni	143	3270	70*	39.40	138.91	0	16
AB de Villiers	120	3257	133*	39.24	149.34	3	21
S Dhawan	113	3082	95*	32.10	121.05	0	25

• Virat's aggregate of 973 runs in IPL 2016 is the highest ever for a batsman in a tournament/series. Before the ninth edition of IPL started, the record of most runs in a tournament/series was shared by Chris Gayle and Michael Hussey with 733 runs – also in IPL.

Virat Kohli in IPL 2016

Score	For	Vs	Inns	Venue	Date	Result
75	RCB	SRH	1	Bangalore	12 Apr 2016	Won
79	RCB	DD	1	Bangalore	17 Apr 2016	Lost
33	RCB	MI	1	Mumbai WS	20 Apr 2016	Lost
80	RCB	RPS	1	Pune	22 Apr 2016	Won
100*	RCB	GL	1	Rajkot	24 Apr 2016	Lost
14	RCB	SRH	2	Hyderabad	30 Apr 2016	Lost
52	RCB	KKR	1	Bangalore	02 May 2016	Lost
108*	RCB	RPS	2	Bangalore	07 May 2016	Won
20	RCB	KXIP	1	Mohali	09 May 2016	Won
7	RCB	MI	1	Bangalore	11 May 2016	Lost
109	RCB	GL	1	Bangalore	14 May 2016	Won
75*	RCB	KKR	2	Kolkata	16 May 2016	Won
113	RCB	KXIP	1	Bangalore	18 May 2016	Won
54*	RCB	DD	2	Raipur	22 May 2016	Won
0	RCB	GL	2	Bangalore	24 May 2016	Won
54	RCB	SRH	2	Bangalore	29 May 2016	Lost

Most Runs in a T20 Tournament/Series

Player	Series	Mts	Runs	Hs	Avg	SR	100	50
V Kohli	IPL 2016	16	973	113	81.08	152.03	4	7
DA Warner	IPL 2016	17	848	93*	60.57	151.42	0	9
CH Gayle	IPL 2012	15	733	128*	61.08	160.74	1	7
MEK Hussey	IPL 2013	17	733	95	52.35	129.50	0	6
JM Vince	NatWest T20 Blast 2015	16	710	107*	59.16	134.46	1	5
CH Gayle	IPL 2013	16	708	175*	59.00	156.29	1	4

- The four hundreds scored by Virat in IPL 2016 are the most by a batsman in a T20 series/tournament. Only other player to score three centuries in a tournament is Michael Klinger – in NatWest T20 Blast in 2015.
- 32.64% of all the runs scored by Royal Challengers Bangalore in IPL 2016 came from Virat's bat, which is the highest percentage of team runs by a batsman in an IPL season.
- Virat has scored four hundreds in IPL (all this year!). Only Chris Gayle – five – has scored more hundreds.
- Virat has played 129 matches for Royal Challengers Bangalore without a break. Only one player – Suresh Raina – has appeared in more consecutive matches for a particular team – 132 for Chennai Super Kings.
- Virat has been involved in three double century partnerships in IPL – most for any batsman.

TWENTY20 MATCHES

- Virat's tally of 6445 runs in T20 cricket is the highest for any Indian player in this format. In fact in all Twenty20 cricket only four batsmen – Chris Gayle, Brad Hodge, David Warner and Brendon McCullum – are ahead of him.

Most Runs by Indian Batsmen in T20 Cricket

	Mts	Runs	Hs	Avg	SR	100	50
V Kohli	204	6445	113	41.85	132.99	4	46
SK Raina	242	6326	109*	33.12	139.00	3	36
RG Sharma	234	6137	109*	33.17	131.13	3	42
G Gambhir	211	5382	93	28.62	120.80	0	44
RV Uthappa	198	5059	92	29.41	132.74	0	26
MS Dhoni	240	4883	73*	37.56	135.90	0	18

Most Runs in T20 Cricket

	Mts	Runs	Hs	Avg	SR	100	50
CH Gayle	257	9151	175*	41.97	150.53	17	57
BJ Hodge	256	6998	106	37.42	131.73	2	46
DA Warner	220	6868	135*	34.86	143.71	5	54
BB McCullum	237	6687	158*	31.54	137.22	7	32
V Kohli	204	6445	113	41.85	132.99	4	46
SK Raina	242	6326	109*	33.12	139.00	3	36
RG Sharma	234	6137	109*	33.17	131.13	3	42
KA Pollard	312	6094	89*	31.25	152.77	0	30

- Virat's tally of 2,096 runs in T20 matches at M. Chinnaswamy Stadium, Bangalore is the highest for any batsman at a particular ground in the shortest format.
- In the year 2016, Virat has scored 1,490 runs at an average of 99.33. Only one batsman has aggregated more runs in a calendar year in T20 cricket – Chris Gayle, 1,665 in 2015.

Most Runs in T20 Cricket in a Calendar Year

	Year	Mts	Runs	Hs	Avg	SR	100	50
CH Gayle	2015	36	1665	151*	59.46	164.52	3	10
V Kohli	2016	29	1598	113	94.00	146.87	4	14
CH Gayle	2012	40	1532	128*	47.87	151.68	3	13
CH Gayle	2011	31	1497	109*	57.57	174.67	4	10
CH Gayle	2013	33	1344	175*	49.77	149.66	3	7
DJ Hussey	2010	49	1275	81*	36.42	133.36	0	7
RN ten Doeschate	2013	44	1248	95*	37.81	148.21	0	8
LMP Simmons	2014	37	1209	100*	37.78	123.61	1	9
DR Smith	2014	44	1203	110*	29.34	129.35	2	7
DA Warner	2011	33	1181	135*	42.17	136.84	3	7

- Virat was involved in 229-run partnership with AB de Villiers for the second wicket for Royal Challengers Bangalore against Gujarat Lions in IPL 2016 – the highest partnership for any wicket in Twenty20 cricket.

Miscellaneous

- Made three double hundreds for Delhi Under-17s.
- Captained India Under-19s to title win in the 2008 Under-19 World Cup in Malaysia.
- Scored 932 runs in 12 Under-19 Tests for India at an average of 51.77 with 3 hundreds and 6 fifties.
- Scored 978 runs in 28 Under-19 ODIs for India at an average of 46.57 with one hundred and six fifties.

(All statistics and records are updated until 31st May 2016)

About the Author

Vijay Lokapally has written on cricket for more than three decades. He is a widely travelled cricket scribe with the distinction of having reported extensively on the game from practically every international venue.

Working since 1986 with *The Hindu*, a respected National newspaper, Lokapally is acknowledged for his insightful views on the game. He covered his first Test in 1981 as a freelancer and has the distinction of covering six limited-over World Cups for *The Hindu* and *Sportstar*.

His enviable access to cricketers, past and present, gives Lokapally a ring-side view of the game in India. He lives in Delhi with wife Sunanda and son Akshay.

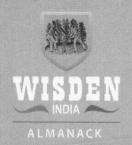

WISDEN
INDIA

ALMANACK

A Joy for Every Indian Cricket Fan

WISDEN
INDIA
ALMANACK
2016

EDITED BY SURESH MENON

Includes contributions
from Sunil Gavaskar,
Richard Hadlee,
Michael Holding, Bishen
Bedi and many others.

Wisden India Almanack 2016	₹699
Wisden India Almanack 2013	₹599
Wisden India Almanack 2014	₹599
Wisden India Almanack 2015	₹799

BLOOMSBURY